SAMUKELISO MOYO

FROM STRUGGLE TO STRENGTH

Finding Inner Strength In Life's Challenges

First published by The Sibanda Iron Soul Series. 2026

Copyright © 2026 by Samukeliso Moyo

All rights reserved. No part of this publication may be reproduced, stored, or transmitted in any form or by any means, electronic, mechanical, photocopying, recording, scanning, or otherwise without written permission from the publisher. It is illegal to copy this book, post it to a website, or distribute it by any other means without permission.

Samukeliso Moyo asserts the moral right to be identified as the author of this work.

Designations used by companies to distinguish their products are often claimed as trademarks. All brand names and product names used in this book and on its cover are trade names, service marks, trademarks, and registered trademarks of their respective owners. The publishers and the book are not associated with any product or vendor mentioned in this book. None of the companies referenced within the book have endorsed the book.

The Sibanda Iron Soul Series™ and the associated Golden

Lion emblem with crown Logo are of Samukeliso Moyo. All rights reserved. First edition.

First edition

ISBN: 978-1-83492-446-5

This book was professionally typeset on Reedsy. Find out more at reedsy.com

Preface

This book was not born in a quiet room with a steaming cup of tea and a tidy desk.

It was born in shacks that shook in the wind, in yards where
I washed clothes until my fingers went numb, and in streets where I collected tins while people who once knew me walked past and pretended not to see.

For years, my story was something other people told for me.

They told it in whispers over fences.
They told it as warnings to their children.
They told it as gossip to entertain themselves.

In their version, I was a "street kid," a failure, an embarrassment, a problem to be managed or pushed aside. None of them knew the full truth. Many did not care to know. But they still spoke with the confidence of people who thought they owned my narrative.

Acknowledgments

My deepest gratitude goes to my parents, who have been my greatest sanctuary through every storm. Thank you for the countless sacrifices you made to ensure my survival and for nurturing me with a love that has been my anchor. Without your unwavering belief in me, I would not have made it this far. Even in the most challenging times, you never met my struggles with blame or harshness; instead, you offered a constant source of strength.

I will never forget that one phone call with my mother—hearing the pain in her voice as she learned of my hardships. Even as she tried to arrange for me to come home, I knew I had to persevere. I held onto the belief that my tears would one day become a testament to our shared triumph. To my father, a true king and the greatest fighter I know: I pray that God grants you both a long life to witness the full harvest of my success.

I also wish to extend my sincere gratitude to the many hands that held me up when I was falling:

- To those who gave me piece jobs: Your belief in the dignity of my work provided more than just a wage; it provided the hope

I needed to wake up the next morning.

- To my clients: To every woman who sat for me so I could plait her hair, trusting my hands even when my heart was heavy— thank you for the exchange that kept food on my table.

- To the providers of shelter: To those who opened their yards and homes with genuine, good intentions, offering my daughter and me a roof without expecting my soul in return.

- To the advisors and truth-tellers: To the friends and neighbours who pulled me aside to offer a word of advice, a warning of a trap, or a spark of hope—your words were maps that helped me navigate the darkness.

- To the "2%": To the rare individuals and families who treated me with fairness and respect, proving that a person's background does not dictate their worth.

Each of you is a part of this story. Whether it was a job, a room, or a simple "don't give up," you were the fuel that kept my light from going out.

Introduction

FROM STRUGGLE TO STRENGTH is my answer to that.

This is my testimony in my own voice.

I did not write this book to make anyone feel sorry for me. I wrote it so that the women who have been overlooked, mislabeled, and silenced can see themselves on the page and realise they are not alone.

If you have ever:

- slept in a room that didn't feel like yours,
- worked until your body hurt and still went to bed worried,
- protected your child with nothing but your body and your will,
- carried shame that was never yours to begin with,

then this book is for you.

I am not a professor of trauma or a polished motivational speaker. I am a woman from Matopo, Kezi, who went to Goholi Primary and Goholi Secondary School, the first born of three children, who loved writing long before she ever held a published book in her hands.

The stories in these pages are not perfect. They are real.

They are stories of being used, discarded, lied about, and laughed at. But they are also stories of small miracles: a plate of food, a safe corner, a kind word, a stranger's job offer at just the right time. They are stories of the iron slowly forming in my soul.

I wrote this book to:

- break the silence around hidden forms of abuse and exploitation,
- honour the "2%" of people who chose kindness over cruelty,
- and remind you that your current situation is not your final identity.

If, by the time you close this book, you feel even a tiny spark of courage to rebuild—whether it's your life, your faith, your self-worth, or your dreams—then my suffering has not been in vain.

This is not just the story of how I was broken. It is the story of how I began to build.

With love and honesty,
Samukeliso Moyo

1

CHAPTER 1

UNSEEN WOUNDS: MY CHILDHOOD STORY

Happiness felt distant during my childhood. I often found myself asking, “Why is this happening to me?” Every experience, every challenge, slowly shaped me into someone I didn’t recognize—like a monster growing inside, born from hurt and confusion.

My home was full of laughter and joy because of my mother. She was a war veteran, strong yet gentle, and she loved us deeply. She made sure we had everything we needed. Her kindness and generosity reached many people, but some took advantage of her. They insulted her, used her, and behaved as if her help was something they deserved, not a gift.

I grew up around my father’s side of the family, and the way they treated us—especially my mother—left a deep, negative mark on me. Their behaviour often made me wonder if life would have been better if we had been closer to my mother's family instead.

My father was unemployed and often went fishing. He struggled with anger because of how others treated him, but my mother's calm nature usually kept him steady. To me, he was strong and protective, like a guardian. Still, he had a quick temper and would often argue over small things. Our home

was a place of love, but it was also a place of tension.

As the oldest of three children, I saw our family life in a way my younger siblings could not. My father had children from previous relationships, but the only one I truly knew was the brother who lived with us. When my mother was home, he seemed kind and helpful. But the moment she left, everything changed.

Whenever she was away, his presence filled our lives with fear. He would stuff us into large bags and beat us hard with sticks and slaps. My younger brother was too little to understand what was happening, but he felt the terror just as deeply. After each beating, we were forced into silence, afraid that any complaint or tear would bring even worse punishment. That life was unbearable.

I often questioned if he was really my brother. How could one person be so different depending on who was watching? In front of my mother, he was gentle. Behind her back, he was cruel.

His behaviour caused my mother great pain. Ironically, people outside the home believed she treated him badly, which was

completely untrue. It made no sense. Why would she mistreat him when our home was always open to others, even to people who were not her own children?

One event still hurts me deeply. My brother lied to my uncle, saying that my mother had refused to give him food. His lie started a big argument between my parents. But the truth came out, everyone there admitted that he had eaten and had even left food on his plate. Watching my mother cry that day was awful. She was suffering because of a lie.

The final straw came when my brother didn't return home until after dark. My mother searched for him everywhere, worried and exhausted. She eventually went to my aunt's house. At first, they all claimed they hadn't seen him. Then, one of the daughters-in-law finally admitted they had been hiding him there. Angry and hurt, my mother left him with them.

His situation there was terrible. He suffered harsh beatings, hunger, and constant insults that made him feel worthless. Desperate for food, he started catching birds just to survive. My mother was afraid of bringing him back home. She feared he would hurt us again. Watching him suffer was painful, but she had to protect her own peace and safety, and ours.

The saddest part was that his own relatives—the people who were supposed to care for him—were the ones abusing him. They had corrupted him, encouraged his bad behaviour towards my mother, and then turned against him too.

After my brother left, my mother often spoke about certain things that stirred anger in me, even though I understood why she said them. She talked about how she had left us in his care many times, and how she always found us unhappy when she returned. One day, she decided to follow her instincts.

She pretended to leave the house but stayed outside, watching through the window. What she saw confirmed her worst fears: our brother questioning us harshly and physically hurting us. When she confronted him, he brushed it off and claimed it was just playing.

But the story that broke my heart the most was another one she shared. She had left us in the care of my brother and a cousin. When she came back, my younger brother was crying uncontrollably, and both of them were nowhere to be found. As she tried to feed the baby, she noticed his mouth was badly burned. That was when she discovered the terrible truth: our cousin had heated a spoon in the fire and forced it into my brother's mouth

After hearing that, I couldn't understand how our own cousin could be so cruel. Eventually, it became clear that their actions weren't just about hurting us as children—they wanted to hurt my mother. They wanted to disturb her peace and break her spirit.

My mother was strict and didn't tolerate bad behaviour. She was tough and would beat us if we misbehaved, but her discipline came from love and a desire to teach us right from wrong. I grew up knowing the difference. Still, I noticed that our relatives reacted very differently when she disciplined us

compared to when she disciplined my brother. When it came to him, they judged her harshly, even though they were the ones feeding his anger and fuelling his disrespect.

My mother's selflessness often led to her being used. She shared everything with our relatives, even when they did not share with her. I remember our scotch-cart, pulled by donkeys. My mother let everyone within relatives borrow it for free. But when it finally broke down and she needed help, one of the same family members who had used it many times actually charged her.

That moment stayed with me. It was one of the first times I truly understood how unfair the world could be to a kind and generous heart.

2

CHAPTER 2

BETRAYAL BY BLOOD

My parents were used by others, and it broke my heart. There was a time one of my cousins came to live with us, and we shared everything with her—even our home. My parents treated her like their own child. But despite all they did, she still kept important secrets from them.

One day, I saw that my mother was unusually quiet and upset. She later told me that our cousin was getting married, and that the lobola (bride price) negotiations were happening at my uncle's house without her knowledge. My mother felt disrespected and excluded, and it hurt her deeply.

At that moment, I began to see the truth: our relatives didn't truly care about us. They were happy to use my parents, but not to honour or include them. No matter how much my parents did, it was never enough.

When the day for the lobola negotiations came, the groom's family didn't show up. Later, our cousin became pregnant and moved in with her boyfriend instead. Only a month after she gave birth, her husband started abusing her and openly admitted that he preferred other women.

When they fought, she didn't run to the people she had shared her happy news with. She ran to my parents. My father went with her to fetch her child and gave her support, along with a place to stay for the day. Once again, my parents were there when life turned dark—but not when things were good.

I felt lost and confused. I didn't know how to react to the harmful relationships in my family. It slowly felt like we were becoming isolated, relying only on ourselves. Every decision our relatives made seemed to cut us off even more, making me feel like we didn't belong. It was as if my parents were tools— used when needed, then put aside when joy or celebration appeared. Being left out of good news and important events only deepened that feeling.

Whenever relatives had problems, my parents were the first ones they called. But when things were going well, we were forgotten. That contrast showed me a painful truth: we were alone in our struggles, with no one truly standing beside us.

In Africa, knowing your family history is important. People believe that not understanding your roots can attract misfortune. Children are taught traditions and expected to follow family rules. But my father grew up without his own father, and that left a hole in his story.

One day, I overheard my parents talking about how my father's family hated him. They spoke about the day his mother—my grandmother—died. My father hadn't been there, and she had left a message for him. No one told him about it at the time. Only years later, as an old man lay dying, did he reveal the truth.

The old man's silence all those years was surprising. When he finally spoke, the message was about my father's own father. Hearing this stirred up many emotions in me. I wondered how different my father's life might have been if he had known his story earlier.

As I tried to make sense of the world around me, I felt helpless watching my parents being taken advantage of. I was too young to give them advice, but their constant sadness and the betrayal around us affected me deeply. It seemed like no one in our extended family truly cared for us, and that lack of love felt like a curse passed down from one generation to the next.

Even at school, I was reminded of this rejection. Strangers bullied me because of things my own family had done or said. They mocked the way I walked and talked, as if my whole being was something to laugh at. Their words made me resent the help my parents gave to people who didn't appreciate it. Their cruelty slowly damaged my self-worth, until I began to hate myself—and even hate God.

I felt cursed, wondering why I had been born with weaknesses that others loved to attack. In my desperation to escape their judgment, I tried to change how I spoke, how I walked, even how I behaved. Even their comments about my clothes cut deep. They laughed at the simple clothes my parents could afford, calling them "old-fashioned." Each insult broke my heart a little more, leaving me feeling helpless and abandoned.

Then, a tragedy shook our community. A young boy drowned in a nearby dam.

As the truth came out, it became clear that his death was suspicious. His friends were warned to stay quiet or risk going to jail. My father, who hadn't gone fishing that week, was fortunate; otherwise, suspicion might have fallen on him.

Still, behind his back, his enemies—including some of our own family—began plotting. My brother was even pressured to lie about my father in exchange for rewards. Thankfully, the truth eventually came to light, though those truly responsible were never fully punished. Two of the people who had tried to frame my father were exposed. The investigation cleared his name, and the case was finally closed.

But the damage had already been done. Everything that happened took a toll on my father's mental health. Things became very serious one day when my mother called us, saying that something was wrong with him. She said he was losing his mind.

I didn't want to believe it, until I saw it with my own eyes. My father, the man I had always seen as strong and protective, was rolling on the floor, crying and saying he wanted to die because his family hated him. That was the first time I had ever seen my father cry.

If I had had the power, I would have done anything to help him. I imagined calling a family meeting, demanding answers, asking them why they hated him so much. What had he done that was so unforgivable?

Over time, I grew to hate my extended family, even though I pretended not to. I didn't want them to know how deeply their actions were hurting not just my parents, but me as well.

In secret, my parents whispered about how happy some of our relatives and enemies would have been if my father had gone to prison. They had built a plan based on lies, never realizing that innocence can still be a shield.

Their twisted idea of justice was to destroy him for no reason, to lock him away and throw away the key. Because of all this, my mother became more and more angry. She often spoke to herself, her words ending in tears.

"Why is this family doing this to me?" she would ask the empty room. "I have done so much for them, but they still treat me like I'm nothing." Whenever she talked to herself, she didn't want anyone around. If someone interrupted, she would get angry.

I often hid nearby and listened, sometimes crying silently with her. I learned that my mother preferred to pour out her pain alone. If our relatives had truly understood how much their actions were breaking my parents, I believe they might have thought twice. But they didn't see it—or they chose not to.

CHAPTER 3

A QUIET CHILD IN A LOUD WORLD

Every pain my parents went through settled inside me like a weight. The drowned boy's case created a deep separation between my mother and her relatives. The little peace we had was gone. Her sister, the grandmother of the boy, came and took all her belongings that were at our home, as if cutting the final tie.

I could see how hard life was for my parents. The only small comfort was that my sister—the mother of the boy who died— and her husband could see that everything was driven by hatred. They even told my father that some of his own family members were pushing them to find a way, true or not, to get him arrested.

As things grew more tense, I started secretly listening to my parents' conversations more often. Each day, I became more aware that my father's family didn't want him—or us. We were his children, but we were not truly theirs.

One evening, I overheard my father telling my mother a story that made fear settle into my bones. He said that after drinking with his uncle one night, he had fallen asleep. Later, he woke up to the sound of people in the community beating that same uncle.

When he tried to defend him, he was shocked to learn that his uncle had been planning to poison him. That was why they were beating him. That night, I went to sleep thinking, "This hatred is deep. It will never end." My parents tried to keep these things between themselves, but I often listened quietly, holding their secrets in my small heart. It was a heavy burden for a child.

I have always been a quiet and thoughtful person. I value my time alone. I like to observe, to think, to stay in my own space. Some people see that and think I'm cold or unfriendly, but the truth is the opposite—I feel everything very deeply. I just don't always show it.

Part of my silence came from being different. The way I walked, the way I talked—people made fun of it. They misunderstood me. It felt like everyone who wanted to feel powerful chose me as their target, because I didn't fight back easily. I was the quiet one, the easy one to pick on.

Day by day, I started to feel like an idiot. My mind was never at peace. I began to struggle in everything—at home, at school, in

my thoughts. It was like I was slowly fading.

One day, on our way home from school, we stopped at the river to play. There was a mix of boys and girls. When it was time to leave, one of the girls realized her pen was missing. We all searched for it, but it didn't turn up. She said she would be in trouble at home because her parents didn't want her playing after school.

I think that's when she decided I would be her solution. Suddenly, she turned to me and demanded that I give her pen back. I was shocked. I hadn't even seen it, let alone touched it. She started pushing me, but I kept saying I didn't take it and tried to walk away. Ignoring the problem didn't help.

She followed me, and her friends began cheering for her to beat me. The pushing turned into hitting, and everyone was laughing. Their laughter cut deeper than the blows. Home was far away, and there was no one to stop what was happening. I tried hiding behind trees, hoping she would give up, but she didn't. Finally, I told myself I had to face her or this would never end.

When I turned to fight back, I realised she wasn't as strong as I had imagined. I hit her until I felt it was enough, and her friends ran away. But the story didn't end there. Her friends insulted me, and her sister promised to beat me in front of my cousins—who were also laughing at me.

At school, the bullying continued. One day, when the teacher asked the class who wet their blankets, a classmate pointed at me, and the room exploded with laughter. I tried to defend myself, but no one stood up for me. The same girl later accused me and another girl of stealing her lunchbox. We were forced to look for it, and it was finally found in the river. To avoid more drama, I walked away, swallowing my anger and shame.

Some children were protected by their relatives, but I wasn't. I couldn't even go to my own family and ask for help with the bullying. I had to face every situation alone. As the oldest child, I felt responsible for protecting my younger siblings, even while I had no one protecting me.

Watching other children being defended by their families made me cry silently. I would ask myself, "Why did I get this kind of family? Why don't I have that kind of protection?"

Heartbreak became a constant companion. It felt like a shadow that followed me everywhere. I reached a point where I couldn't even smile. I was trapped in a cycle of deep sorrow, replaying the same painful memories in my mind over and over. I didn't know how to speak up for myself or to say what was hurting me, and that silence made everything worse.

My vulnerability made me an easy target. People blamed me for things I hadn't done, and I carried those accusations like they were true.

While I was still trying to process my pain, something happened at school that shattered me even more.

One day, my younger brother was sick and couldn't go to

school. The next day, I was called to his classroom. His teacher immediately demanded to know why my brother had been absent. I calmly explained that he hadn't been feeling well and had stayed home.

Instead of listening, she slapped me.

In front of a classroom full of younger children—including my own brother—she asked me again, "Why was your brother not at school yesterday?" I stood there, stunned. I couldn't understand what I had done wrong. Why was I being hit for explaining that my brother was sick?

I stayed quiet for a moment, then repeated my answer: "He wasn't well. He was at home." She slapped me again, even harder. The blow was so strong that I saw stars, and tears filled my eyes. My own mother had never hit me that hard. For a moment, one of my ears went almost deaf.

Afraid of being hit again, I lowered my voice and gave her the answer she clearly wanted to hear—that my brother had been hiding from school. She insulted me in front of everyone, calling me names while the children laughed.

Then she sent me back to my class and beat my brother as well. I felt responsible for his pain, even though I didn't know what else I could have done.

The rest of that week was a nightmare. The story spread through the school like a joke. Some students laughed at the visible mark of her hand on my face—a red reminder that stayed there for nearly a week. I felt lost, humiliated, and completely alone, drowning in misery and wondering if my life would ever be different.

CHAPTER 4

DARK ROADS AND HIDDEN SCARS

It felt like bad luck followed me everywhere. One day, while walking home from school with my cousin who has since passed away, we met a dangerous man hiding in the bushes. He grabbed me, threatened to do terrible things to me, and described what he wanted in words no child should ever hear. I was just a young girl in primary school, far too young for his sick desires.

Just when I thought something horrible was about to happen, a stranger appeared from nowhere and the evil man ran away. That moment still makes me shake when I think about it. Even now, I wonder what would have happened if that stranger hadn't been there. That day, I realised just how powerful God's protection can be, even when no one else sees what you're going through.

After that, the man kept watching me. I saw him often, especially when I went to or came from school. I began to hate school because it felt like the source of so much of my pain. Sometimes I would see him ahead on the road, and I would run to the other side, closer to the houses where I felt safer. I once heard him telling his friend that he would catch me one day. Those words echoed in my mind.

The near attack destroyed my sense of safety. I struggled to focus in class because my mind was always somewhere else—on that bush, that man, and how vulnerable I really was. I kept asking myself, "Why would an older man target me?" I had no answers. Fear ruled my thoughts and affected my everyday life. At home, I felt restless, worried, and alone.

I was completely terrified and didn't tell my parents. In my mind, I imagined how the community might react, how people might twist the story and somehow blame me. So I kept quiet. I hid my thoughts and my fear. I cried when I was alone and asked myself why I was being punished. I started avoiding people and changing my routes. I learned to walk where there

were more houses and fewer quiet paths.

My teachers didn't notice the change in me, as long as I showed up at school. Inside, I was falling apart. I became afraid of walking alone in quiet areas and often hid or arrived late, hoping to avoid danger on the way.

This behaviour slowly took over my life. Even when I was punished physically for being late or hiding, it didn't change how I felt. The memories of that day haunted me. I simply couldn't cope.

To make things worse, a boy in my class bullied me constantly. He used to put biting ants down my uniform, making me wriggle in discomfort during lessons and hate school even more. I finally told my father, and he stepped in and stopped the bullying. That was one of the few moments I felt seen and defended.

Still, most of the time, I went through my struggles alone. No one noticed how much emotional pain I was in. I felt invisible, as if no one could see I was hurting. Even those who were supposed to protect me didn't always do so.

Embarrassment, bullying, and sadness became my daily life. I started to hate myself and even my home, as if they were the reasons I had so many problems. I tried to be strong, but inside I was breaking.

Some teachers, without realising it, made things worse. They thought they were correcting or disciplining me, but their harshness only deepened my fear of school. I began to arrive late more often or hide to avoid them, which only led to more beatings and punishments. I understood that actions have consequences, but it didn't feel fair when no one saw what I was really going through.

One particular day still haunts me. I arrived late at school and was beaten in front of my classmates. The teacher didn't give me a chance to explain. She just beat me without mercy. I fell to the ground, humiliated and in pain. After school, a classmate

made fun of me, and I became the joke of the day.

That evening, I sat near my parents' house and thought about ending my life. I felt completely hopeless. I didn't know why I was alive or what my purpose was. Everything felt heavy and pointless. But then I thought about my parents and how much it would hurt them if I were gone. I couldn't do that to them. Somewhere inside, a small voice reminded me that I still had many years ahead of me and that maybe, just maybe, things could get better.

So I chose to keep going.

Despite everything—the bullying, the fear, the shame—I finished school with good grades. I was genuinely proud of myself for that. Looking back, I saw a girl who was breaking inside but still refused to completely give up.

From these experiences, I learned important lessons:

– Bullying is never okay. It can cause deep, lasting damage. Iam living proof.
– I must stand up against bullying whenever I see it.

– I must stay away from bullies and teach my child never tobecome one.

– I must make it clear that I do not approve of bullying in anyform.

– Speaking out and not suffering in silence is the path tohealing and freedom.

Those dark years tried to destroy me, but they also planted the seeds of the person I am becoming—someone who understands pain, and someone who refuses to ignore it in others.

CHAPTER 5

THE WEIGHT OF BULLYING

Secondary school was supposed to be a fresh start—a new chapter on my path to becoming a doctor. I dreamed of helping people, of changing lives. But life had other plans, and instead of hope, I was greeted by humiliation and pain.

On my first day, I arrived in a uniform that was far from perfect. It was the best my struggling parents could afford during very hard economic times. My blouse was old and slightly seethrough, and I felt exposed and ashamed before anyone even spoke. My books were carried in a flimsy plastic bag because we couldn't afford a proper school bag. That plastic bag became another symbol of my vulnerability.

It didn't take long for the mockery to begin. My uniform became a joke, and my bag made me an easy target. Sometimes, my books were stolen straight from that plastic bag, forcing me to rewrite notes and assignments from the beginning. On days when my parents couldn't afford to replace what was taken, I faced beatings from teachers for having incomplete work. They never asked why. They only saw what was missing, not the story behind it.

The bullying didn't stop at classmates. When a relative of mine started attending the same school, I hoped it would mean support. Instead, it became another source of pain. That relative joined in the mocking and insults, especially about my uniform. Hearing it from the family cut even deeper. I felt powerless, trapped in a world where even my own blood added to my shame.

One day, a girl pushed me so hard from behind that a window broke. I hadn't done anything, but I was near the window. That was enough for the teachers. I was blamed along with the girl who pushed me. We both received a beating and were forced to share the cost of repairing the window. Once again, I paid for something that wasn't my fault.

The same girl constantly slapped me and insulted me. She even warned me that if I fought back, she would refuse to eat until she died—twisting the situation to make me feel guilty and afraid to defend myself. Her words were strange and cruel, a way to control me without touching me.

Eventually, I reached a point where I couldn't take it anymore. One day, when she tried to bully me again, I stood my ground.

I fought back. For the first time, I didn't just accept the pain. I

protected myself. People might call that a victory, but inside, it didn't feel like one. I knew I had to fight, but something in me still felt uneasy. Violence, even in self-defence, didn't sit comfortably in my spirit.

Outside of school, life was no easier. Our community was struggling with hunger and poverty. My parents were war veterans, and when food aid or support came, their status was often ignored or forgotten. During times of high inflation, when government help was rare and small, even people who were not as close to us received more support than we did. We went hungry often, while my parents did everything they could with the little they had.

My mother's strength during this time was a light in the darkness. At one point, things were so bad that she even considered cooking painted seeds—seeds we all knew were poisonous— just so we would have something to eat. That thought alone shows how desperate things had become. Sometimes, the small amount of food I received at school became our shared meal at home. I would bring it back, and my mother and I would quietly share it. It was a small meal, but it carried a big message: love, sacrifice, and survival.

As if poverty and bullying were not enough, the atmosphere in our community grew even more dangerous. There were people who terrorized us, threatening my mother's life because they believed she supported another political party. They used rumours and accusations as weapons. Their hatred was deep and frightening.

We began to live in constant fear. Some days, we had to hide to protect my mother. Sometimes we stayed at my aunt's house, trying to stay out of sight, waiting and hoping the danger would pass. But even in hiding, the fear followed us. It felt like they would eventually catch us no matter where we went.

Despite all our hiding, the sense of being hunted never fully left. The hatred from these people made it seem like being captured or attacked was only a matter of time. That fear lived in my chest like a second heartbeat.

Relief finally came when my father returned from work. He saw what was happening and decided he wouldn't allow it anymore. He confronted the people who were threatening my mother. His presence, his courage, and his refusal to back down brought a sudden end to the open harassment. The same people who had terrified us went quiet.

For a while, his strength silenced the violence and fear that had swallowed our days.

Under all this—bullying, poverty, threats, and emotional scars— I was just a young girl trying to survive. And even though I didn't see it clearly then, each painful moment was shaping a version of me who would one day be able to tell this story, and use it to help others feel less alone.

6

CHAPTER 6

ABANDONED AND INVISIBLE

My world felt like it was falling apart. It seemed like nobody loved me, and almost no one even noticed I existed—except when it was time to hurt me. Everyone I met seemed to bring pain without a second thought. I felt completely alone, living only for my parents and my siblings.

I tried to fit in, but every attempt brought more sorrow. I didn't know how to cope. Then came a sports event at another school, far from home. I went as a spectator, surrounded by kids from my area and many others. For a moment, it felt like I was part of something normal.

When the event ended, we all started the long journey back. As people were dropped off, the group grew smaller.

Eventually, only the children from my neighbourhood were left. Once they were sure their own loved ones were safe, they looked at me and made it clear that I was on my own.

Two boys got on bicycles and carried two girls, leaving me to walk alone in the dark.

Tears streamed down my face. I was in an area where a man had once tried to harm me, and all I could pray was, "Not today, God. Please, not today." I walked home in the darkness, unable to see who was in front of me or behind me. My heart ached with one painful question: "Where am I going, when no one loves me?"

I had to cross a bushy, lonely area, and I cried as I walked, wondering how I was supposed to make it alone. Then I saw a figure standing ahead of me and froze, thinking, "Just another bad day." But then a voice called my name.

It was my mother.

I ran to her and told her everything. She didn't say a word, but I could see the pain in her face. It was a deep, quiet sadness that came from our poverty and from knowing she couldn't give me the protection and comfort other children had. She loved me deeply, but love doesn't always erase the reality of hardship.

That night, I replayed every moment in my mind. Why would people treat me so cruelly? "Shouldn't I be safe?" I asked myself. "Is this really the life I'm meant to live? Why don't people feel any remorse?" The experience made me hate school even more.

I kept wondering, "When will this end? When will I find peace?

CHAPTER6

When will my parents have enough money for me to live like everyone else?"

I didn't know then that these painful lessons were slowly building the woman I am today.

I became a target. Fear followed me everywhere. I isolated myself, my trust in people completely shattered. Others laughed at my pain while I endured it in silence. While other children seemed to have everything, I ached for simple things my parents couldn't afford.

I remember longing for the beautiful hats sold at school. Every time I mentioned them, my mother would listen quietly, knowing we didn't have the money. Still, she found a way. One day, she bought me a cheaper hat and a pair of socks. It might have seemed small to others, but to me, it was a huge victory. I felt seen.

That morning, hope filled me. "Today, I will wear something special," I thought. I was excited to get to school early and feel like a new person, even just for a day.

But my joy didn't last long.

On my way to school, a boy on a bicycle sped toward me. I tried to move out of his way, but he swerved and hit me directly. I fell to the ground, the world going blank for a moment. When I opened my eyes, he was standing over me. There was no concern on his face, no apology—only arrogance.

He called me names and even tried to hit me again. Shocked and overwhelmed by pain, I stayed silent. He grabbed my new hat, the one my mother had sacrificed to buy, dusted himself off, and tossed it to the ground. It landed covered in grease and dirt, ruined.

He warned me to "watch where I was going" or he would hurt me even worse next time. Then he left, as if nothing had happened.

I forced myself to stand, my right foot throbbing with every step, and continued walking to school. On the way, I met a group of girls. I told them what had happened and said I wanted to report him. Instead of supporting me, they laughed.

"Just forget it," they said. Their words cut deeper than the fall. To them, I was just a poor girl from a poor family. They told me my parents would never stand up to him, so reporting it was pointless. Their laughter made me feel like a joke. "Just forget everything and move on," they said, as if my pain meant nothing.

When I got home, my mother could see that something was wrong. But I knew my father's reactions too well. I didn't want to bring more trouble or stress into the house. So I lied. I pretended I was fine, even though my heart was breaking.

That lie pushed me further away from school in my mind. I started to believe that education was for other people—not for someone like me. I went to school only to avoid disappointing my parents, not because I believed it held a future for me.

CHAPTER6

Deep down, I felt trapped in my own personal prison. Every time I looked at my uniform, I wanted to tear it to pieces. I convinced myself that it was the uniform—the symbol of school, of poverty, of bullying—that was the source of all my struggles.

What I didn't see then was that even in those moments of feeling abandoned and invisible, I was surviving. And survival, in a world determined to break you, is a quiet kind of strength.

7

CHAPTER 7

DENIED EVEN WATER

One day, I went to fetch water near my uncle's place. Something small turned into a big dispute, and suddenly we were denied access to the water. His daughter-in-law's anger exploded. As I tried to walk away, she grabbed me, beat me, and then, out of pure spite, threw away the water I had worked so hard to collect.

It was "just water" to her, but to us it was life. That incident left me shaken and anxious for a whole week. It was another reminder that even in the simplest things, we were not safe from cruelty.

My mother did her best to care for us with the little we had. Our clothes were often old and worn, but she would carefully mend them, stitching them back to life with her hands. To us, it was a necessity. To some of our relatives, it was a joke.

They mocked our patched clothes, laughed at the signs of our poverty. Their words stung, but beneath the shame, I felt a quiet pride in my mother's resourcefulness. Her hands turned "nothing" into "something," and that was a kind of dignity they would never understand.

All the hardship and hatred around us weighed heavily on me. One day, I asked my parents why life seemed so hard for our family. That's when they shared a painful story from my father's past.

During the war, my father had been captured. He was taken back to his own community, and the people there were asked if they knew him. Afraid, and wanting to protect themselves, they denied knowing him. That denial nearly cost him his life. He was saved only because one brave schoolgirl stepped forward and told the truth.

Hearing this shook me. Even in the face of death, his own people had refused to stand with him. Realising that even family and community had once turned their backs on my father brought tears to my eyes. It made sense of the coldness we were living in—but it also broke my heart.

After that, I began to withdraw into myself more and more. I stayed home when I could, avoiding drama and gatherings. I felt like an outsider, someone who had no true place in the world, no circle where I fully belonged.

Hardship seemed to invite more hardship. At school, there were meal programs, but hunger was still a constant companion. Sometimes the food wasn't enough. Sometimes it didn't reach us at all. My empty stomach made it hard to think, hard to focus. Lessons became a blur. My grades dropped, and eventually I had to repeat a year. That meant starting again with a new group of classmates—and a new wave of bullies.

One boy in particular targeted me relentlessly. He had beat me with a stick while the rest of the class laughed. The pain in my body and the humiliation in my heart felt unbearable. To avoid him and others like him, I began skipping classes whenever a teacher wasn't present. I knew that if I ever tried to fight back, it would only bring worse consequences.

I felt trapped in a cycle I couldn't escape: hunger, poverty, bullying, shame. It was like being caught in a storm with no shelter in sight. And yet, somewhere deep inside, a small spark of hope refused to die. I still wanted more from life. I still

wanted to rise above it all.

School had once been a symbol of hope for me—a place where I thought I could grow, learn, and move toward my dreams. Instead, it had become a battleground. Each day there chipped away at my confidence and self-worth.

Home, however, remained my sanctuary. No matter how hard things were, there was love there. Acceptance. A place where I was not a joke, not a target, but a daughter. Even with little food and many problems, home was where my heart could finally breathe.

CHAPTER7

Despite everything, I stayed in school. I pushed through the fear, the humiliation, the laughter, the hunger. I finished. That simple fact is one of my quietest but greatest victories. The scars of those years didn't disappear—but they shaped a strength in me that nothing and no one could take away.

After school, wanting to do better and learn from my past mistakes, I went back to repeat my last grade. I was denied. No access. No help. Deep inside, I suspected that my poor attendance and lack of focus in the past—things rooted in bullying and trauma—had marked me in their eyes.

It hurt. The wounds from those years still felt raw.

The constant bullying had slowly crushed my dream of becoming a doctor. I had wanted to help people, to heal others. Instead, I found myself stuck at home, watching others move forward while I remained in the shadow of everything I had gone through.

Over time, I began to understand something important: my story wasn't just mine. Many children suffer in silence. Some experience deep trauma, including sexual abuse or near-abuse, and carry it alone. These experiences consume their thoughts and leave them feeling like death is the only way out. Fear keeps them quiet. Their behaviour changes, their school performance suffers, and sometimes they become angry or violent—but beneath it all, there is pain that no one has asked about.

Bullying is not just "kids being kids." It is a devastating force that can turn a child's life into a living prison. It attacks their identity, their hope, their sense of safety. Some never recover. Some end their lives. Some hurt others. I am deeply grateful that I survived my own experience, and because of that, I feel a strong responsibility to speak up.

If you ever see a child showing cruel behaviour, intervention is not optional—it is necessary. Left unchecked, that behaviour can grow and turn them into the kind of person who destroys others.

Schools must be safe places, not torture chambers. They should be spaces where children learn, grow, and feel protected—not where they are beaten, mocked, or broken. Teachers have a powerful role. When they see bad behaviour, they must not ignore it. They must ask questions, listen, and act to protect all students.

Despite the setbacks, I chose to rise above my past. I decided to adopt the spirit of a soldier—wounded, but still standing. I became determined to build a better future for myself.

Through this long, painful journey, I learned to stand up against injustice, to value small joys, to lean on God even when I didn't understand His plan, and to keep pursuing my dreams, no matter how many times they seemed to die.

My story is not just one of suffering; it is a quiet triumph. A reminder that even in the darkest places, a small light can survive—and that light can guide others out of their own darkness too.

8

CHAPTER 8

GROWING PAINS AND HARD LESSONS

Life after school felt like standing still while everyone else moved forward. Other people were finding jobs, starting new lives, and making plans. I stayed at home, lost and idle, with no idea what to do next. No one showed me a way forward. My parents were already overwhelmed by their own struggles and the battles with family and enemies. They had no clear solutions for me either. I felt stuck, useless, and left behind.

In my loneliness and desperation for stability, I entered a relationship. At first, it felt like hope. My partner seemed supportive and caring. He even bought me a new phone, and I treasured it—it felt like a small symbol that I finally mattered to someone.

But slowly, things began to change. He became distant and cold.

I kept wondering what I had done wrong. Every time I tried to ask, the conversation went nowhere. His silence became its own kind of answer.

The truth cut deeper than I imagined. I discovered he was seeing one of my relatives. At first, I didn't want to believe it. But then I saw it with my own eyes—his picture as her phone wallpaper. It was like a punch to the stomach. The pain grew sharper when I realised he had bought her the same type of phone he'd bought for me.

It wasn't just betrayal; it was humiliation.

Even though I had chosen not to be intimate with him, the emotional betrayal shattered me. My days turned into long stretches of tears and silence. I felt grief like death inside me. My body changed. My mood changed. My mother noticed I wasn't myself, but I couldn't bring myself to tell her what had happened. It felt too shameful, too heavy to say out loud.

I felt like I was dying slowly on the inside, asking myself if I was just born to fail—at love, at life, at everything.

Time passed, and the pain softened just enough for me to move again. My uncle's son helped me find a job as a shopkeeper at a general store that sold alcohol and groceries. I was excited. It felt like a fresh start, a chance to stand on my own feet.

But the job was harder than I imagined.

I worked with two other girls, one of them the manager. The

hours were long, and rest was a luxury. We slept very little, often trying to catch up on sleep during the day or in between tasks. I shared a room with one of the girls, and her boyfriend visited often. Their loud, intimate moments made me deeply uncomfortable. I tried to pretend I was asleep which wasn't helping. I then had to quietly leave the room to the kitchen,

which wasn't safe at night.

The door was never locked, and every sound at night made my heart race. I knew anything could happen while I slept there. I was constantly on edge, worried about being attacked. But I had no better option.

One day, while I was in the kitchen, a woman noticed how I was living and seemed concerned. She offered to help me find a safer place to sleep. Relieved and grateful, I saw her as an angel. She took me to her house and gave me a place to rest. I thought my prayers had finally been answered.

But her kindness took a dark turn.

She left me alone in a room with a man who she said would do my hair. At first, it sounded like a favour, a nice gesture. But as the evening went on, it became clear that his intentions were not innocent. When it grew late, he refused to leave the room and said it was "too late" for him to go.

I was terrified.

I refused to undress. I stayed awake the whole night, watching his every move. He made repeated sexual advances, trying to pressure me, but I kept saying no. I warned him that I would report him if he tried anything. The tension in that room made every minute feel like an hour.

When morning finally came, I grabbed my things and ran back to work, shaken and angry. In my panic, I had forgotten my phone. When I returned for it, they refused to give it back at first. I reported what had happened to the police, and after some resistance, I eventually got my phone.

That experience haunted me. It made me feel like nowhere was safe—not home, not work, not even in the care of someone who seemed kind at first.

Out of fear and confusion, I did something I'm not proud of, but at the time it felt like survival: I decided to find a boyfriend for protection. In my mind, choosing someone myself—where I had some control over intimacy—seemed safer than being at the mercy of men who might overpower me.

A man showed interest in me, and I hoped he would keep me safe. Later, I discovered he was married. I hadn't known. That truth broke whatever fragile hope I had left. Still, at that time, it felt like the only "shield" I had.

Eventually, my boss called me into his office. He accused me of sharing “shop secrets,” even though everything he mentioned was public knowledge. Then he confronted me about dating a married man. I felt blindsided and ashamed. Before I could fully process what was happening, I was fired.

That night, I had to sleep there one last time, in the same uncomfortable room, and they refused to give me even a blanket. One kind co-worker quietly lent me one, and I never forgot that small act of humanity.

The next morning, I could see the cost of his kindness. His boss insulted both of us, using harsh words and showing clear anger that he had dared to help me. I stood firm, refusing to let them see me break.

I left that place with my dignity, if nothing else. A woman I considered like a sister had given me support and advice during that time, and with her encouragement, I returned home—back to the same familiar feeling of stagnation.

About a month later, terrible news reached me. The same supportive friend who had helped me and guided me had died from food poisoning. I was devastated. It felt like any time I found someone kind, life found a way to take them away.

I thought about her often. I replayed our conversations, her strength, her laughter. I wondered if I might have shared her fate had I stayed there longer. Her death felt senseless and unfair, another reminder of how fragile life can be.

Back at home, I once again found myself entangled in family drama. My desire to escape—to live far away from all of it—grew stronger. My mother's kindness continued to be used against her. Watching people take advantage of her hurt me deeply.

One incident stands out. My aunt borrowed a small amount of money from my mother to help with a cultural ceremony related to her son's pregnancy. She promised to pay it back quickly. A year passed. When my mother finally asked for her money, my aunt insulted her, accusing her of witchcraft simply because she had asked at night.

All this over ten dollars.

The argument escalated beyond reason. It wasn't about the money anymore. It was about respect—and how little of it my mother received. I knew in my heart that my real family, the ones who truly cared, were my parents and my siblings. But that was a truth I couldn't openly say without causing more conflict.

Accusations of witchcraft against my mother had become painfully common. Even a cousin's son, someone she had helped, threw those same words at her. That kind of betrayal is hard to describe. It's like watching someone stab the very hands that fed them.

Over time, the family's open hatred and resentment became almost embarrassing. The closer we were supposed to be, the more obvious their dislike became. Their behaviour made it clear: they wished we would just disappear.

As I grew older, I began to accept this harsh reality. It still hurt, but it no longer surprised me.

One morning, my uncle's daughter invited us to help harvest maize in her fields. I saw it as a chance to maybe reconnect, to feel included for once. When we arrived, she greeted and hugged everyone—except me. She skipped over me as if I wasn't there.

I felt a wave of shame and rejection wash over me. With no way to get home alone, I stayed and helped with the work, my heart heavy and my spirit bruised. The whole time, I kept asking myself, "Why did she invite me if she didn't even want me there?"

It felt like a deliberate act of humiliation. Another reminder that even in family spaces, I was treated like an outsider.

And yet, through all of this—betrayal, disappointment, humiliation—I was still here. Still standing. Still learning the hard lessons that would one day become the foundation of my strength.

9

CHAPTER 9

TRIALS IN BOTSWANA

Life at home had become a standstill. I wanted to move forward, to build something of my own, but I felt stuck and dependent on my parents. My independence was trapped by poverty and lack of opportunity. Desperation grew inside me, and the house that once felt like a sanctuary started to feel like a cage.

Then an unexpected invitation came—from Botswana. It felt like a small light in a very dark tunnel. I didn't have a passport, so the idea of crossing the border was risky and frightening. But staying where I was felt even worse. So I took the risk.

I joined strangers and crossed the border illegally. We hid, ran, and moved in fear, constantly looking over our shoulders. Every sound felt like danger. The emotional scars of that journey stayed with me long after we reached the other side. Still, even with all the fear, I chose to be resilient. I told myself that stepping into the unknown was better than drowning in despair.

When I finally arrived at my brother's house, my body showed the price of the journey—scratches, aching muscles, and sheer exhaustion. The next day, we travelled again, this time to my sister's place. As she picked me up, people warned us that police sometimes arrested those on the streets without proper documents. The sight of any officer sent shivers down my spine. I realised just how much trouble desperation had pushed me into.

I prayed silently for us to arrive safely, and thankfully, we did. In my heart, I knew: border jumping is dangerous. Many people have lost their lives trying to cross. May their souls rest in peace.

After a long time of being unemployed at my sister's house, I finally found a job—something I had begged God for. At first, I
was excited. It felt like my breakthrough.

But very quickly, the environment began to feel wrong.

My employer carried a deep sadness, like a permanent shadow on her face. She rarely smiled. Her cold demeanor and sharp, watchful eyes made me uneasy. Whenever her husband was expected home, her actions ordered me to stay inside, away from him. The tension in the house was thick.

I started to wonder: if she didn't trust me near her husband,

why did she hire me at all?

After only two months, she dismissed me without explanation. She said she would call me again, but that call never came. Everyone around us was shocked; no one understood why I was let go. I had tried my best. Deep inside, I couldn't help but ask myself if it was because of my slow speech, my walk, or simply because I was different.

Time passed, and another job offer came. I accepted, hoping for something better. Instead, it turned into a nightmare.

The work was heavy and endless. I was hired to care for a disabled woman, but the duties went far beyond that. The pay was small and unfair for the amount of responsibility I carried. My days were twelve-hour shifts with no proper breaks, full of physical labour and emotional strain.

They had a washing machine, but they made me wash huge piles of laundry by hand every week, no matter the weather. Cold, heat, or rain—it didn't matter. I scrubbed clothes until my hands burned, developed sores, and my feet went numb. Only brief moments in the sun gave me a bit of relief.

In the morning, I had to tidy their bedroom, which they left in a terrible state. Sometimes I found used condoms under their pillows and on the floor. Cleaning that mess made me feel degraded, like I was less than human. I felt more like a prisoner than an employee.

Basic freedoms didn't exist there. I wasn't allowed to watch TV.

My phone was also a problem. One day, my employer saw me with it and demanded it. I apologised and put it away, trying to avoid conflict. Still, the message was clear: they wanted control over every part of my life.

Their romantic displays in front of me were constant and uncomfortable. No matter how much I tried to look away, it was impossible to ignore. It often felt like they enjoyed watching me squirm.

I ran errands at night, walking in fear and praying for protection. On one of those nights, some homeless boys actually helped me find my way safely. Their kindness stood in sharp contrast to the cruelty of the people I worked for.

Another evening, I was sent to buy Pampers after the shops had already closed. When I returned empty-handed, she insulted me, calling me useless and poor. No matter what I did, it was never good enough.

One day, she asked me to fetch something from her room. When I saw her husband inside, I hesitated at the door. Before I could explain, she grabbed me, pushed me into the room, and there he was—completely naked. She then slapped me and shoved me back out, as if I had done something wrong.

I counted the days to payday like a prisoner marking days on a wall.

They claimed to be Christians and forced me to attend church with them. But at church, they would eat while I sat at the back,

watching. They never shared. Their words spoke of God, but their actions spoke of pride, control, and cruelty.

Even on my rare days off, they left piles of dirty dishes and messes that waited for me. Their tolerance for filth—but only when I was around to clean it—was shocking.

When the month finally ended, I was ready. I had quietly packed my things. On payday, my salary was short by P200. When I questioned it, they said it was because my performance was poor. The injustice burned. I knew how hard I had worked. The job was already underpaid, and now they were reducing it even more.

That was my breaking point.

I quit.

A wave of relief washed over me as I walked away. The place that had felt like prison for a month and a half was finally behind me. But the trauma didn't disappear overnight. Back at my sister's house, I still felt haunted. Certain TV channels triggered memories of what I had gone through. Nightmares and flashbacks followed me into sleep.

Slowly, life offered me a softer chapter.

I found a third job, and this time, things were different. My new employers were kind. They treated me with respect. For the first time in a long time, I felt peace in my workplace. May God bless them for the way they cared.

As Christmas approached, I wanted to go home. At first, we planned to do a border jump again. On the way, the police stopped us. We were fined P200 each and given papers that allowed us legal passage. Even with that, some in the group chose the old route—the risky one.

I followed them, even though I knew the danger.

We walked through the bushes in broad daylight, tired and thirsty. Every step felt heavy, but something in me kept pushing forward. Eventually, we reached the home of one of the girls. We stayed there for the night, resting our aching bodies, gathering strength for the final leg of my journey home.

I had left home in desperation and returned with scars—but also with lessons, strength, and a deeper understanding of just how much I could survive.

10

CHAPTER 10

FLEEING ONE NIGHTMARE, FINDING ANOTHER

South Africa called to me like a promise—a new land, new chances, a place where maybe my life could finally move forward. I arrived with my passport, a hopeful heart, and the desire to connect with my mother's family. I told myself I was leaving old hardships behind, stepping into a fresh start as a newcomer.

At first, it seemed like things might finally be different. One of my cousins welcomed me warmly, even buying a cake to celebrate my arrival. For a moment, I felt seen and valued. But the warmth didn't last long.

Other relatives were cold and distant. Their eyes held no welcome. At night, the house was filled with the sound of arguments between my cousin and his wife. Their constant fighting shattered any sense of peace I hoped to find there.

Looking for a calmer place to stay, I moved in with another female cousin. But peace still didn't come.

Her husband complained constantly about food and rent. Every little thing became a problem. Even when I tried to help, it never seemed enough. One grocery trip stands out in my memory: I went shopping on an empty stomach, tired and hungry, doing my best to carry the heavy bags and make sure I didn't forget anything. Instead of gratitude, I returned to complaints.

My cousin's moods were unpredictable. One night, out of nowhere, she kicked me out. I stood outside in the dark, waiting, unsure what I had done wrong. Eventually, she let me back in, but the damage was done. I felt unwanted and unsafe. I held on to the small hope that maybe my uncle, one day, would offer me a more stable home.

A child of my aunt visited once, saying she was just passing through. She offered no comfort, no real support. My cousin's husband took that chance to cut me even deeper with his words. He pointed out how no one from my own family had come to stand by me. Knowing how my father's relatives might treat me if I ran to them, I realised I truly had nowhere else to go. I had to stay strong on my own.

His favourite answer to everything was, “It’s my house.” He used those words to shut down any feeling I might have, any attempt to explain. My cousin tried to excuse his behaviour by saying, “He’s a man, that’s how they are.” But that explanation

didn’t soften the blow. His insults about how I had no real ties to him, no power, no right to complain, cut straight to my heart.

Even another cousin’s brother rejected me, saying I wasn’t family and he didn’t know me, despite the fact that we shared the same uncle. That rejection hurt deeply. In a foreign country, they were the only relatives I had, and they made it clear I didn’t belong.

While I stayed with them, I was unemployed. I tried to contribute by taking care of the house and helping my pregnant cousin. But even that came with constant complaints and criticism. It felt like nothing I did was ever good enough.

In the middle of all this darkness, there was one bright light: Nkululeko.

We met online, and his kindness stood out from the coldness around me. I began to see him as a brother. One day, when I had nothing to eat and no one to turn to, he sent me money. That small act of kindness felt huge. It reminded me that not everyone in the world was cruel.

Eventually, I found a well-paying piecejob. It felt like a turning point. With my first salary, I helped with some of the household expenses where I was staying. It felt good to finally contribute.

When my second paycheck came, my heart turned homeward. I wanted to send money to my parents, who had sacrificed so much for me. But when I mentioned it, my cousin disapproved. She told me that when she had once lived in South Africa, she never sent money home to her parents and implied I shouldn't either.

I understood her story, but I knew my heart. My parents had stood by me through everything. I chose them.

So I sent the money secretly.

After my cousin gave birth, things in the house became even more tense. Our landlady and her relatives threw a loud, disruptive party right outside our door. There was no consideration for the newborn baby. When we complained, they brushed us off, saying, "The baby can't hear or see anything yet."

The disrespect turned into an argument that escalated quickly. That night, they did something unthinkable: they removed our door while we were sleeping.

We reported it to the police, hoping someone would help. But the landlady proudly told us that her daughter had "friends" in the police. Nothing was done. We were on our own.

The harassment grew worse. The landlady's daughter insulted us constantly and even physically attacked me. The next day, the landlady herself beat me with a broomstick. My fingers throbbed with pain. That night, with no door to protect us, a rat bit my foot. The pain was unbearable. That was the final sign—we had to move.

We left that place behind, but the emotional weight stayed.

I felt lost and alone in a foreign land. I didn't want to worry my parents or add to their burden, so I tried to appear strong from a distance. Inside, though, I was breaking. I began to count my tears, telling myself that one day, they would be proof of how much I had survived. I repeated to myself, "This too shall pass," like a prayer.

Then, another female cousin invited me to stay with her. I took that as a small sign of hope and accepted.

She herself was not the problem, but her husband was abusive. He shouted at her, insulted her, and beat her—even in public. Watching it filled me with anger and helplessness. I wanted to defend her, but his aggressive nature made it too dangerous to confront him.

One day, he grabbed scissors and came at us in rage. At that moment, I knew that staying there would eventually cost us more than just peace—it might cost us our lives.

Again, Nkululeko stepped in. Aware of my situation, he helped me find a job as a caretaker. With that opportunity, I also helped my cousin escape her abusive marriage. We left together, and I finally felt a sense of relief and purpose. For once, I wasn't just surviving—I was helping someone else survive too.

But even that victory was short-lived.

After we escaped, my cousin asked me to buy her a new phone. I had spent almost everything I had to help us get away. I was still using a broken phone myself. I explained that I didn't have the money.

Her reaction was cold and ungrateful. She became angry, as if everything I had done meant nothing because I couldn't give her what she wanted next. It cut me deeply. I had risked and sacrificed when others, who were safer and richer, did nothing.

She had once promised to always be there for me, but as soon as she was safe, she pulled away. Her distance and ingratitude felt like yet another betrayal.

From that experience, I learned something important: human loyalty can be fragile and temporary. People can love you loudly in one moment and abandon you quietly in the next. But God's faithfulness is different. It doesn't disappear when times become easy or hard.

In the middle of rejection, abuse, and disappointment, my faith remained the one constant thread. It didn't erase the pain, but it reminded me I was never truly alone.

11

CHAPTER 11

THE DATING EXPERIMENT

I thought dating might finally bring the stability I craved—a chance to build my own family while my parents were still alive to see it. As the eldest, I felt a heavy responsibility to secure my future, to stop being a burden and become someone who could stand on her own feet. But every step I took into the world of love seemed to open a new door to pain and lessons I never asked for.

While working, Cynthia and Peter—became my close circle. We supported each other through stress, loneliness, and the everyday grind. Over time, Peter began to show more than friendly interest in me. I noticed how he spoke positivity into my life, how he encouraged me when I felt small. His presence, at first, felt like a blessing.

Peter worked hard moulding bricks, a job that demanded everything from his body. His hands were rough, his clothes often dirty, and his face carried the tiredness of long days in the sun. People sometimes made unkind comments about how he looked—how worn and older he seemed. But I chose to see past that.

I saw his effort. His work ethic. The quiet care he showed me and others.

So when he suggested we date, I agreed—but with a clear boundary. We decided we would wait before becoming intimate. That choice made me feel a bit safer, like we were building something slowly and intentionally.

We grew close quickly. We were always together, and people started asking me what I saw in him. Their words carried judgement, aimed at his appearance and status. But I was used to being judged myself, and I wasn't going to allow the same thing to be done to him. I became protective. I stood up for him. I refused to let anyone speak badly about him in my presence.

He would visit me, and we'd spend our evenings watching TV together, sharing simple moments. Those small routines started to feel like the beginning of a real relationship, something stable to hold on to.

Then everything broke.

One evening, while we were watching TV like usual, he changed.

Without warning, he forced himself on me. I tried to fight him off, but he was stronger. He overpowered me and raped me.

In that moment, the boy I had defended, trusted, and believed in became someone else—a stranger who took from me what I had clearly said I wanted to protect.

Afterwards, he apologised, saying he didn't know what had come over him. But no apology could undo what had been done. The word "sorry" felt empty compared to the weight of what I now carried in my body and soul.

The worst part was the silence that followed.

Because everyone knew we were in a relationship, I felt trapped. I imagined the comments, the blame, the questions: "Why were you alone with him?" "But he's your boyfriend." "Are you sure?" The thought of reporting him felt impossible. So I buried the truth inside myself. I walked around with a deep, silent wound that no one could see.

About two weeks later, I noticed changes in my body. I felt different. Something inside me whispered that this wasn't just stress or illness. I went online, searching for answers, and slowly a chilling suspicion formed: I might be pregnant.

I told him what I suspected. To my surprise, he didn't run. He bought a pregnancy test and stayed with me as we waited for the result.

It was positive.

CHAPTER11

Seeing that result felt like the ground had disappeared beneath my feet. I was torn. I hadn't wanted a child like this—conceived through pain, without my consent being respected. But the thought of an abortion also weighed heavily on my heart. I was scared of the physical risks, the spiritual weight, and the emotional consequences. After many silent struggles and prayers, I decided to keep the baby. It didn't feel like an easy choice—but it felt like the only one I could live with.

Throughout my pregnancy, he showed support. He attended to my needs, talked about our future, and kept saying he was single, that I was the one he wanted to build a life with. His remorse for what he had done seemed genuine. The way he took responsibility for the baby softened some of my anger, even though the scar of that night never truly went away.

Slowly, I began to wonder if I could give him a second chance.

Maybe this was our story now—broken, but repairable. I thought about our child and how much it needed both parents. I thought about how hard it is to find someone who at least tries to stay. So I opened my heart again, bit by bit, hoping this time he would honour it.

He kept working hard, saving money. Eventually, he told me he had saved enough to open his own shop. Hearing that filled me with a new kind of hope. I imagined a real future: a small business, a steady income, a home for our child, and maybe, finally, some stability.

I knew my job was temporary and poorly paid, but his business felt like a door opening—a possibility that we might one day stand on solid ground, not just surviving, but actually living.

I allowed myself to dream again.

I pictured us as a family. I pictured bringing our baby into a place where we didn't have to beg or depend on anyone. For the first time in a long time, the future didn't look completely dark.

What I didn't yet know was that this "dating experiment" still had more painful lessons to teach me.

12

CHAPTER 12

THE DARK SIDE OF MONEY

Money, I came to learn, can be a powerful and dangerous force. It doesn't just tempt the poor; it can twist the hearts of people who already have more than enough. Greed, I realised, doesn't care about status or position. It simply feeds on opportunity. I was about to experience this truth firsthand.

At the time, I was working as a home caretaker. My salary was small, but I was genuinely grateful for it. It gave me some dignity, a sense that I was contributing and building something, even if slowly.

Then my fragile peace was broken.

Out of nowhere, my cousin demanded R400 from me, insisting that I owed them money. Their explanation was weak and confusing. Deep down, I knew it wasn't right. But I also knew how quickly conflict could explode in my family. I was tired. Tired of fights. Tired of being the problem. So I swallowed my anger, forced myself to be calm, and paid the amount.

On paper, the debt was "settled." In my heart, it wasn't.

I felt drained and deeply frustrated. That R400 wasn't just money—it was food, transport, future plans, a tiny bit of progress. Watching it disappear over a lie made me feel like my efforts were pointless. Under their influence, success felt almost impossible, as if every step forward would be dragged backward by someone else's greed.

I began to pray more honestly and more boldly: asking God to give me a life far away from their negativity, and the strength to stand on my own. I made a quiet promise to myself—I would rely on my own effort and refuse to let their selfishness define my future.

Not long ago, my boss's wife had introduced something that sounded hopeful: a stokvel—a savings club. She explained that if I contributed R200 every month, I would receive a big share of groceries in December. For someone who had known hunger, that sounded like security. It felt like one small, smart step toward stability.

I joined.

CHAPTER12

Month after month, I contributed faithfully, even when it meant tightening my belt.

Then, in November—just one month before the payout—my boss's wife suddenly dismissed me. Her reason: financial difficulties. I was pregnant and had just lost my job, with no warning and nowhere secure to go. I had no choice but to move in with Peter. It wasn't the future I imagined, but it was the only shelter I had.

When December came, I went to claim my stokvel groceries— the ones I had paid for with my sweat and sacrifice.

Instead of a simple handover, I walked into chaos. My boss's wife started crying dramatically, turning herself into the victim and stirring up her husband's anger against me. It was as if I
was asking for something that didn't belong to me.

Eventually, they pretended to "help," offering me a ride part of the way home. But along the road, they dropped me off and left me there—in the dark. Pregnant, abandoned, and carrying the weight of yet another betrayal.

Peter came to fetch me from where they had left me stranded. I refused to let things end like that. We went back with the police to confront them. Once they realised the law was involved, their bravado disappeared. Fearing legal trouble, they finally released my groceries.

But the story didn't end there.

The man who had originally helped me get that job—Nkululeko—somehow got pulled into my boss's wife's lies. Her manipulation turned him against me. It broke my heart, because he had once been a source of kindness and support.

He had been holding my groceries for me and kept urging me to collect them. But I was struggling financially and logistically. Sending the groceries home to my parents was complicated and expensive, and no one, not even Peter, offered to help me make it happen.

Meanwhile, Nkululeko complained about space and rats, saying the groceries were in his way. His tone changed from concern to pressure. I felt cornered, ashamed, and powerless. Eventually, overwhelmed by stress and unable to face more tension, I switched off my phone.

In the end, I lost the groceries.

Everything I had contributed. Everything I had fought for. Gone.

I was left heartbroken and betrayed—by my boss's wife, by the system, and even by someone I had once trusted deeply.

The whole ordeal was excruciating. My boss's wife had taken advantage of my vulnerable situation as a pregnant woman, fully aware that I had limited options and no real protection. It was more than financial abuse; it felt like a deliberate act of cruelty.

CHAPTER12

I cried for a week. Not just for the groceries, but for what they represented—lost effort, lost trust, lost hope.

But I didn't have the luxury of staying broken. I was carrying a child. I had to find a way to stand up again, even with shaking legs.

From this painful chapter, a few hard truths carved themselves into my heart:

- In dark times, real friends are rare.
- People's true intentions can stay hidden until money isinvolved.
- Trusting others always carries risk, especially when youhave little and they have power over you.
- Money doesn't change everyone—but it can reveal theugliest parts of some people.

The old saying that “money is the root of all evil” suddenly made painful sense. I had seen how it could twist kindness into manipulation, opportunity into exploitation, and relationships into transactions.

But I also knew this: even in the middle of greed and betrayal, I was still learning, still surviving, and slowly becoming wiser about who and what I gave my trust to.

13

CHAPTER 13

RESILIENCE BORN: MY JOURNEY TO MOTHERHOOD

Life's uncertainty forced me to narrow my focus: my relationship, and the little life growing inside me. Even though our finances were fragile and the future unclear, something inside me refused to collapse. A quiet resilience carried me from one day to the next.

For a while, Peter's shop felt like our lifeline—a sign that we might actually build a stable future for our child. Then everything started to crumble. One day his employee stole from the business, and the loss hit us hard. The shop struggled to recover. What had looked like a solid foundation suddenly felt shaky and unreliable.

The weight of responsibility for our unborn child pressed

heavily on my heart. I worried constantly about how we would provide: food, clothes, a safe home. As Christmas approached, the shop's problems only deepened. Instead of joy, there was tension and fear. Still, I held on to hope. I kept praying that things would turn around.

For a moment, it seemed like they did. There were small improvements, a bit more money coming in, and I allowed myself to breathe again. But that sense of relief didn't last long.

Six months into my pregnancy, the truth I never expected finally surfaced: Peter was married.

The world seemed to stop.

The man I had trusted, defended, and chosen to build a family with already had a wife. The discovery tore through me. I felt betrayed, humiliated, and foolish all at once. It wasn't just a lie— it was a whole hidden life. Deep inside, I felt an icy warning: if he could hide this, what else was he capable of hiding?

Around that time, my sleep became haunted by strange and vivid dreams.

In one dream, Peter left me for another woman. He drove away in a white car, and I was left behind, dressed in torn, old brown clothes. I was pushed around in a wheelbarrow like someone who had lost their mind, chased away by faceless people. I felt unwanted, discarded, and completely powerless.

In another dream, I was carrying a baby girl on my back, trying to move forward through thick, heavy mud. Every step was a struggle, but the people around me moved easily on dry ground, passing by without helping. I was stuck, fighting alone, trying not to fall with the baby on my back.

I shared these dreams with Peter, hoping he would see them as warnings, or at least take my feelings seriously. He brushed them off as "just dreams," nothing to worry about. But to me, they were more than that. They felt like messages, hinting that the road ahead would be filled with difficulty.

His response in real life matched his attitude toward my dreams—dismissive and stubborn.

As my pregnancy advanced, Peter grew more neglectful. He stopped paying attention to my needs. The shop, once our shared responsibility, became dirty and disorganised. Instead of stepping up, he became lazier and more condescending.

So, with my pregnant belly growing heavier, I cleaned the shop, served customers, and tried to keep things running. I pushed myself physically and emotionally, even as his attitude made me feel more and more alone.

Then, one morning before dawn, my world was shaken in a way I will never forget.

I was resting, exhausted from the long days and the strain of pregnancy, when a group of robbers broke into our home. They stormed in with violence and threats. One of them pointed a gun straight at my head. Fear flooded me, cold and paralyzing.

CHAPTER13

They demanded money, searching and ransacking everything, convinced we had something hidden.

Their cruelty didn't stop at threats. They taunted and insulted me, and one of them stepped on my pregnant belly. The pain shot through my body like fire. At that moment, I feared not only for my life, but for my baby's.

Eventually, as the first light of dawn began to break, they fled. I was left behind on the floor—shaking, in agony, and terrified.

Gathering every bit of strength I had, I forced myself to stand. Somehow, I made my way to the clinic. The nurses and doctors attended to me, but the pain did not let up. My body, already stressed and tired, could no longer hold on.

At eight months pregnant, I went into premature labour.

Despite everything—the stress, the violence, the fear—my baby fought her way into this world. Against all odds, she was born healthy.

In that moment, the weight of every hardship seemed to fall away, replaced by overwhelming joy and relief. I called my parents with the news. I could hear the happiness and gratitude in their voices. It felt like light had finally pierced through years of darkness.

I named my baby girl Happiness.

Her name was not just a word; it was a declaration. She was my reminder that even in the middle of chaos, God could still bring beauty. She was the joy that rose from the ashes of fear, betrayal, and pain.

This chapter of my life taught me more than I ever imagined:

That even when everything is collapsing, faith can hold you together.

That resilience isn't loud—it's quiet, stubborn strength that refuses to give up.

That life, no matter how it arrives, is a precious gift.

My journey to motherhood was not soft or easy. It was marked by fear, heartbreak, and violence. But it was also marked by miracles, protection, and a love so deep it gave me new reasons to live.

And in the centre of it all was Happiness—my daughter, my reminder that light can still be born out of the darkest nights.

14

CHAPTER 14

SHATTERED BONDS: A MOTHER'S QUEST FOR JUSTICE

Motherhood transformed my world. Every part of my life began to revolve around my baby's needs. I treasured the quiet moments—watching her sleep, feeling her tiny body relax against mine as I breastfed her, sensing the indescribable bond growing between us. She was my anchor in a stormy life.

But even in those tender moments, a knot of unease lived inside me.

Whenever I left her alone with Peter, something in me tightened. Each time I returned, I would hear stories of how much she had cried. Her inconsolable tears, whenever she was left in his care, awakened an overprotective instinct in me. I tried to silence my worries, but they never completely went away.

One morning, everything shifted.

I woke up to the sound of my baby screaming—a desperate, frantic cry. When I looked over, Peter was holding her. She was naked, with only her Pampers still on, even though I had dressed her fully before we slept.

Confusion crashed into me. Before I could ask what had happened, his belt came down on me with violent force. He beat me, accusing me of being a careless mother, shouting that she had cried while I was sleeping. His words didn't match his actions. As her father, he should have comforted her, protected her, and supported me. Instead, he chose violence.

Then, as if nothing had happened, he left for church.

I was left standing there with my crying baby and a storm of questions and dread. Something was deeply wrong. And a thought, cold and sharp, rose in my mind: "This man is hiding something—and he might be dangerous to my child."

From that point on, our relationship began to crumble in ways I could no longer ignore.

Even though the shop was doing well—largely because of my hard work and effort—Peter grew more distant. A silent resentment began to show in the way he moved, spoke, or sometimes refused to speak at all.

CHAPTER14

He started washing his own clothes separately. Then he began cooking his own food, leaving me to fend for myself. These might seem like small actions, but to me they felt like walls being built, brick by brick, between us.

Then came the final blow.

He told me he wanted me to leave.

In that moment, he revealed the truth he had been hiding: he had a wife. She will be joining him in South Africa soon. I stood there, stunned. The man who had told me he was single, who had spoken of being tired of single life, who had built a future with me and our child—is saying this.

The realization hit me like a physical attack. Every memory of his words replayed in my mind, now twisted by the truth. All the signs I had ignored, all the doubts I had pushed aside, came rushing back as regret and anger.

I remembered my two recurring dreams, the ones I had once tried to brush off. Now they returned with painful clarity.

In one, he left me for another woman, driving away in a white car while I was left behind in torn brown clothes, pushed around in a wheelbarrow and chased away like I was nothing. In the other, I struggled through thick mud with a baby girl on my back while everyone else walked by easily. Those symbols now felt undeniable—warnings I had not fully understood.

We moved to his family's home, which at first had seemed like a safe place. But once there, I began to feel their deceit too. I sensed that they knew all along. Piece by piece, I realised they

were part of a plan: to keep me close only until his wife arrived, then push me out of the way.

Whenever I questioned anything, they denied it with intensity that only made me more suspicious.

Then, barely a month later, another truth came out—one that shattered what little hope I had left.

Peter didn't just have one wife. He had two.

The pain of that discovery was almost unbearable. I cried until my body felt empty and weak. Week by week, I could see the change in my own reflection. The stress and heartbreak were written all over my face.

Peter's indifference made everything worse. He moved through the days as if my pain was invisible. The man I had once known—the one I thought I loved, the father of my Happiness— had disappeared. In his place stood someone cold, detached, and cruel.

I felt like an intruder in his life, a problem he wanted to get rid of. He made no effort to hide his irritation with me. Every word, every look, every silence told me one thing: I was no longer wanted.

Trapped, without any immediate way out, I felt myself sinking into despair. The man who was supposed to be my partner had

used me, lied to me, and then discarded me. His timing, waiting until after our child and after using my labour in the shop, felt calculated and heartless.

One morning, he demanded all the shop's earnings and spent the money on his two wives without a second thought for me or our child. That was the moment something in me broke. The weight of betrayal, exhaustion, and loneliness became too heavy.

In my darkest hour, I tried to end my life.

I didn't see a way forward. I didn't see a way out. All I saw was pain.

But somehow, I survived that moment. And survival itself became a quiet act of rebellion—for myself and for my daughter.

Then, Peter brought his younger brother to take over the shop. He told me clearly I was not allowed to help there anymore. I stayed silent. I was too tired to argue, too drained to fight over what should have been a shared responsibility.

His brother didn't last long. He began stealing from the business and eventually disappeared completely, leaving Peter with losses and problems. Faced with the mess, Peter came back to me—not out of love, but out of need. He apologised and asked for my help.

A small part of my old self responded. I chose to forgive him that much and helped him again with the shop. Not because he deserved it, but because it was in my nature to save what I could.

But even with my help, his resentment didn't fade. If anything, it grew stronger. I finally saw the truth: my presence was more than just unwelcome—it annoyed him. He no longer saw me as a partner or even as the mother of his child. I had become a burden in his eyes.

That was when my resolve hardened.

I knew I had to leave. Not just emotionally, but physically. I needed to stand on my own feet—for my sake and for Happiness.

Finding work became my new mission. I knocked on doors, asked around, faced rejection after rejection. Each "no" added to the pressure, but I kept going. I didn't have the luxury of giving up. My daughter depended on me. She was my reason to wake up, to try again, to push through the fear.

I was no longer just a woman trying to survive love and disappointment.

I was a mother on a mission—to fight for a safer, better future for my child, even if I had to build it completely from scratch.

15

CHAPTER 15

A MOTHER'S HORROR: THE UNTHINKABLE DISCOVERY

Motherhood had already reshaped my heart, but nothing could have prepared me for the day my entire world shattered.

I had gone out briefly to fetch water, leaving my little girl in Peter's care. When I returned, I heard her before I saw her— crying in a way I had never heard before. It wasn't a normal cry. It was deep, raw, and desperate, as if her small body was trying to scream a truth she couldn't put into words.

I rushed to her.

What I discovered changed everything.

As I examined her, a chilling realization washed over me: my baby had been violated. Molested. In that single moment, the pieces I had been trying not to see suddenly fit together. The unease I felt when leaving her with Peter. Her constant crying in his presence. The way my spirit never fully rested around him.

The truth hit me like a physical blow:I was living with a monster.

I refused to look away.

I went first to his relatives, hoping for support, protection, or at the very least, concern for my child. Instead, they dismissed me. They suggested that "anyone" could have done it, as if that made it less urgent, less real. Their denial felt cruel. I understood at that moment that I couldn't rely on them for help, only for excuses.

I went to a private doctor to confirm what I already believed in my heart. Then I took the hardest step: I reported the case to the police.

At the first station I went to, I was turned away. They claimed it was "not their jurisdiction" and showed no urgency, no real care that a baby had been abused. Their indifference stung deeply, but I refused to give up. Eventually, I was transferred to another police station.

This time, I was received with compassion.

At the second station, a policewoman named Brenda listened, cared, and supported me. She became a small but powerful light in that dark time, determined to help us. Ironically, the first station later admitted they were wrong and asked me to return—but by then, their incompetence and coldness spoke louder than their apology.

That night at the police station, everything felt overwhelming.

I had nothing with me—no change of clothes, no nappies, no basic supplies for my daughter. She was distressed and wet herself, the rain outside pouring down as if echoing our misery. I was cold, exhausted, and emotionally broken, holding my child and wondering how this could be happening.

Then, in the middle of that chaos, a stranger became an angel.

A kind woman noticed my distress and came over to ask what was wrong. I shared my story with her—through tears, shame, and shaking hands. She listened, then quietly offered me money to buy nappies for my baby.

It was a simple act, but at that moment it felt enormous. Her kindness gave me a small piece of dignity back. May God bless her for that.

The next step was the hospital.

Accompanied by an officer from the supportive station, I went to seek medical evidence of what my daughter had endured.

But instead of protection, we encountered something darker.

Two people arrived, claiming to be CID officers. At first, they appeared concerned. Then their tone changed. They began insulting me, throwing xenophobic remarks, undermining my story and questioning my worth. They tried to make me feel small, foolish, and powerless. The officer who had come with me stood by, saying nothing.

It felt like another betrayal by those who were supposed to defend justice.

Only the quiet confirmation from the nurses—that something had, in fact, been wrong—gave me a sliver of comfort.

I was later transferred to a bigger hospital, hoping for a more professional and fair examination. The next day, determined not to let prejudice stop me, I went again to seek proper care and confirmation.

But when I arrived, I met four individuals who were not properly licensed, yet claimed they would "assist" us. When

I explained what had happened, they immediately insisted on inspecting my daughter's private parts—without any clear authority, explanation, or proper medical credentials.

I refused.

I was not going to let just anyone touch my child under the guise of "help," especially when I sensed something was wrong. My refusal angered them. They began to threaten that if I didn't comply, they would deny my daughter any help.

Then they took it further.

In a cruel, humiliating act, they took my baby's clothes and exposed them outside, publicly, as if to punish me. Whatever dignity I had left felt stripped away. I stood there, broken, humiliated, and helpless, and I burst into tears. It felt like the whole system was punishing me for daring to speak up.

When I finally saw the doctor, things didn't get better.

He treated me with contempt, questioning my parenting and dismissing my fears. He said he "saw nothing wrong," brushing off my concerns as if I were exaggerating or imagining things. It didn't matter that I was a mother who knew her child. It didn't matter what we had already seen and felt.

I walked out of that hospital not just disappointed—but deeply wounded by a system that seemed more interested in avoiding responsibility than protecting a child.

I began to fear not only the people in my home but the ones in uniform and white coats too.

I wondered how I would ever face my community. I imagined the whispers, the blaming, the judgment—directed not at the abuser, but at me, the mother who dared to speak.

Part of me wanted to disappear.

But a stronger part of me remembered why I was fighting: my daughter. She was innocent. She deserved justice, protection, and a chance at a life not defined by this horror. So I held on to one belief: if I kept standing in the truth, God would fight for us, even when people failed us.

During all of this, Brenda continued to check on us. She called repeatedly to ask about the progress of the case. Her persistence was a blessing. But I was exhausted, afraid that telling her everything would only lead to more pain and more disappointment. Sometimes I held back, not because I didn't trust her, but because I felt like I had nothing left to give emotionally.

Peter often answered her calls instead. He lied, telling her that everything had been resolved, that there was no longer an issue. His words isolated me even more, blocking help that might have reached us.

I went back to the police station again, connected to social workers, and had to relive my story. They asked questions, but my mind felt distant, heavy, weighed down by fear and uncertainty. The so-called CID officers never truly pursued the case. Their neglect stood as a silent reminder of the corruption and cowardice I was up against.

Then, in one final act of cruel sabotage, Peter stole the medical papers—our crucial evidence.

Without those documents, I felt stripped of the little proof I had. It was like he had reached into my hands and taken away my last weapon in this battle.

I was left with my child, my truth, my God—and very little else.

But even then, one thing remained unbroken: my love for my daughter and my determination, no matter how tired or scared, to keep trying to protect her.

16

CHAPTER 16

FEAR, ESCAPE, AND THE ROAD TO EMPOWERMENT

At some point, the truth settled over me like ice: I was being deliberately manipulated. The people and systems I had turned to for justice were not there to protect me or my daughter. Corruption seemed to run through the very structures that were meant to defend the vulnerable.

I realised that if I kept pushing through "official channels," I might not only lose the case—I might lose our lives.

That realization left a scar on my soul. It was more than disappointment; it was betrayal. I had looked for protection and found indifference, cruelty, and danger instead. The trauma of that time became a constant shadow, following me everywhere.

Staying in that house, surrounded by the same people who had covered for Peter, excused him, and dismissed what was done to my baby, felt like living inside a wound that never closed. But I had nowhere else to go—no home, no family nearby, no safety net.

On top of the pain, I had to face humiliation.

The community believed Peter's lies. His charm and manipulation, combined with their prejudice, led them to see me as the problem. I was labelled a liar. Their stares were sharp, their whispers loud even when their mouths were closed. I could feel their judgment in every step I took.

I became hyper-alert. Everywhere I went, I watched people's faces, watched their eyes. I kept my daughter close, shielding her from their cruelty, all while planning silently: one day, we
would leave.

One woman in particular was especially harsh. She spoke about me with disgust, passing judgment as if she were pure and perfect. I had no one to defend me. No one spoke up on my behalf.

In a moment of anger and desperation, I used what I knew.

Her own friend—someone related to Peter—had shared some of her secrets with me. In public, when she mocked me again, I spoke those truths out loud. I exposed what I knew, not out of malice, but from a desperate need to defend myself for once.

I regret it now. But at the time, it felt like the only weapon I had.

Peter's relative, upon hearing what I had said, was instant and violent. Enraged, she attacked me. In front of Peter, she beat me—physically assaulting me while he stood nearby, laughing. My pain was entertainment to him.

When it was over, my eyes were swollen, my body bruised, and my spirit even more battered.

I went to a friend's house, hoping for comfort and shelter, but she wasn't home. Exhausted, with nowhere to go, I spent the night in her toilet—cold, cramped, and alone. I sat there waiting, shaking from pain and fear, wondering how my life had come to this.

The next day, my need to protect my daughter drove me on.

I found an old, abandoned shack—a broken structure, barely fit for living. But to me, it was something precious: it wasn't his house. It wasn't their space. It was a place where, however hard, I could start to separate our lives from the nightmare we'd been trapped in.

That shack became the setting for a new, even harsher chapter.

We had no food. No proper bedding. No real security. I was still breastfeeding, and my own body was weak. Every day

was a battle to find something to eat, something to cover us, somewhere to draw strength from. There were moments when all I had to give my daughter was the warmth of my chest and the sound of my voice.

But that bond with her—the way she clung to me, trusted me, needed me—became my anchor. She was my reason not to give up.

In that broken place, with almost nothing left, I began to gain something priceless: wisdom.

From all of this, certain lessons carved themselves into the deepest parts of me:

I learned the importance of boundaries—clear, firm lines that protect me and my child from people who mean us harm, no matter who they are or how close they claim to be.

I learned the power of empathy—how many people suffer silently behind closed doors, judged by those who know nothing of their pain.

I learned the necessity of self-reflection—looking honestly at my patterns, my choices, and how I could grow stronger and
wiser without blaming myself for what others did.

I learned the courage of truth-telling—speaking up about abuse, even when my voice shook, and even when others tried to silence or shame me.

I learned the freedom of forgiveness—not as a way of saying "it was okay," but as a way of releasing the poison of resentment that could have destroyed me from the inside.

I learned to trust my instincts—that small inner voice that had tried to warn me so many times before. Now, I knew I had to listen to it.

And most of all, I learned the strength of independence—standing on my own, even when my legs trembled, and slowly rebuilding a life that belonged to me and my child.

To anyone reading this who recognises themselves in my story— trapped in a cycle of abuse, manipulation, or fear—I want to say this from my heart:

Leave before it's too late.

Don't wait for:

- The next insult that chips away at your self-worth.
- The next bruise on your body or on your spirit.
- The next broken promise that leaves you shattered.

Pay attention to the red flags:

- Words that tear you down instead of build you up.
- Any form of physical harm or intimidation.
- Control, manipulation, and isolation disguised as "love."
- Selfishness and narcissism that make you feel small andinvisible.
- Cheating and lies that destroy trust and safety.

You are not powerless.

Reclaim your life, your dignity, your freedom:

- Seek professional help—counsellors, support groups, NGOs,anyone trained to help.
- Trust carefully. Let time and consistency reveal who isgenuine.
- Speak, even if your voice trembles. Silence only protectsabusers.
- Believe that healing is possible. Freedom is not just a dream.It is a path you can walk, step by step.

You deserve:

- Love that nourishes, not destroys.
- Respect that honours who you are.
- Safety that lets you sleep at night.
- The freedom to live truthfully, without fear.

My story also exposes something bigger than me: the darkness that can live inside systems meant to protect us. Police officers who mock instead of help. Medical staff who dismiss victims instead of listening. Institutions that turn their backs on the most vulnerable.

It is a painful, terrifying reality—that those in power can sometimes fail us completely.

But even in the middle of all that failure, there is still hope.

There are still good people, like Brenda, like the woman who bought nappies, like the strangers who quietly help. There is still a God who sees what is done in secret. There is still a way forward, even when it begins in an abandoned shack.

And there is still you—breathing, reading, surviving—stronger than you know.

17

CHAPTER 17

FINDING FAITH IN STRENGTH AND RESILIENCE

The weight of everything my daughter and I had been through pushed me to the very edge of my mind. It felt like I was standing on a cliff, with madness and despair pulling at my feet. A suffocating darkness settled over me. Depression wrapped itself around my thoughts, and the only thing keeping me from falling completely was a thin, fragile thread of resilience.

I came to understand that depression is a dangerous enemy. It doesn't just make you sad; it twists your thoughts, distorts reality, and makes even simple decisions feel impossible. My mind was trapped in a loop—replaying the trauma, the betrayal, the poverty, and the fear, over and over again. Our harsh living conditions only made everything worse.

In that darkness, suicidal thoughts began to creep in—quiet at first, then louder.

But every time I thought about giving up, one image pulled me back: my daughter. This small, innocent child I had fought so hard to protect. She became my anchor, the one unshakable reason to keep living, even when everything in me wanted to disappear.

I slowly withdrew from the world.

I locked myself and my baby into our tiny, broken space. I avoided people. I avoided questions. Even the simplest tasks— bathing, eating, moving—felt too heavy. Some days, I went without food. Some nights, I stayed awake till morning, my mind racing, my body exhausted, tears refusing to stop.

I became a mother who was always crying.

Anger began to grow inside me too. I was easily irritated by any noise, any disturbance. I wanted silence, complete silence. I wanted to exist in a world where no one asked anything from me.

In that raw, hurting state, my daughter sometimes became the unintended target of my frustration. In moments of emotional overload, I snapped at her, raised my voice, or reacted harshly— and the guilt that followed was immediate and crushing.

Each time, I was reminded of a painful truth: I was the only parent she truly had. The only one who could protect her, especially after what her father had done. Hurting her, even with words or impatience, cut me deeply. I hated myself after those moments, even when I knew they came from my own brokenness, not from lack of love.

Days melted into each other.

I could feel myself drowning in despair, sinking deeper and deeper. Then, in that dark place, a hard realization surfaced: no one was coming to save me. I was my own lifeline.

My body began to show what my heart and mind were going through.

I lost weight. My clothes hung loosely on me. Standing up too quickly made the room spin. Weakness followed me everywhere. I had starved not just my spirit, but my flesh. I felt like a shadow of myself.

But even as my body weakened, my instinct as a mother refused to die.

I pushed myself to feed my daughter, even when I didn't eat. Spoon by spoon, I gave her what I could. My own appetite was gone, but my responsibility to her was not. Her little life was the flame I kept trying to protect against the wind.

Over time, the emotional pain began to show up as physical illness too.

Hunger became a constant ache. My stomach hurts often. I felt sick, drained, and fragile. My body was crying out for help, even when my mind struggled to care.

Then a terrifying clarity came: if I didn't get help soon, my daughter might lose me. And if she lost me, who would protect her?

So, with what little strength I had left, I took the hardest step.

I walked to the clinic and told them the truth: about the depression, the darkness, and how far I had fallen. I didn't hide behind "I'm fine" anymore. I allowed myself to be seen as I really was—broken, exhausted, and desperate.

The staff listened. They examined me with care and compassion. I received medication and a small, precious gift: a chance to heal.

It wasn't instant. Healing never is.

But slowly, day by day, I felt tiny shifts. A bit more energy. A moment of clarity. A few minutes without tears. I held onto every small improvement like a lifeline and told myself, over and over:

I must heal.
I will heal.

I made a decision: I would not let the insults, gossip, or judgment of others define me. People could call me crazy, broken, dramatic—whatever they wanted. They hadn't walked in my shoes. I chose instead to focus on my own growth, my own strength.

Some people passed through my life with temporary help or concern. But I often sensed a quiet doubt in their eyes, as if they weren't sure I was stable or sane. That hurt, but I refused to let it stop me. I knew what I had survived. I knew what I was fighting for.

I turned intentionally toward positivity.

I surrounded myself with what light I could find. Gospel music became my refuge. I played songs that spoke of hope, faith, and God's love. The lyrics wrapped around my heart like a blanket, reminding me that I wasn't completely alone, even when I felt abandoned by people.

As the medication began to work and the fog in my head slowly lifted, I started to re-engage with life—one tiny step at a time.

First, small chores. Washing a few dishes. Sweeping the floor. Straightening our space. Then, eventually, I began going outside more, letting the sun touch my skin, feeling the air on my face. Each step was a quiet act of resistance against depression.

I also began taking better care of myself.

I forced myself to bathe regularly, even when I didn't feel like it. I tried to eat what I could, even if it was simple or small. I treated these acts not as luxuries, but as survival tools—ways of telling my mind and body, "You still matter."

The more I leaned into faith and positivity, the more I noticed change.

The dark cloud didn't vanish overnight, but it grew thinner. My reactions became calmer. My thoughts became clearer. I could look at my daughter and feel not just pain and fear, but hope again.

The world around me didn't suddenly become kind.

People still whispered. Some still looked at me with judgment, as if I would forever be the woman they saw at her lowest point. But I had changed. Inside, I was no longer begging for their approval.

I began to stand taller—not because my past disappeared, but because I no longer let it define my entire identity.

I held onto one unshakable belief: God had been with me in every dark room, every tear, every sleepless night. Even when I felt abandoned, I now see that something kept me from fully breaking. That something was His hand, and the strength He planted inside me.

My journey through depression wasn't just a story of suffering. It became a story of:

Courage to ask for help.
Strength to keep going when I wanted to stop.

Faith that refused to die, even when everything else did.

I was not "back to who I was before"—I was becoming someone stronger, wiser, and more compassionate. Someone who could one day turn all this pain into purpose.

18

CHAPTER 18

RISING ABOVE ADVERSITY

Peter brought his wife to South Africa. Hearing that news hit me like a physical blow. It felt like watching all my hard work, sacrifice, and hope being handed over to someone else. The old saying echoed bitterly in my mind: “A fool’s hard work is enjoyed by the wise.”

The pain dragged me back toward the familiar darkness of depression. It was as if the whole community was silently watching, entertained by my suffering, while I stood alone in the middle of it, exposed and humiliated.

Stress became my constant companion.

I replayed Peter's behaviour over and over again: his coldness, his lies, his ability to move on as if nothing had happened, his lack of gratitude for everything I had done. Whenever I tried to remind him of how deeply he had hurt me, he would respond with a dismissive, "Everything has its timing," as if my pain was just a passing inconvenience.

Those words cut deeply. They reminded me that, to him, my feelings did not matter.

As my situation grew more desperate, my thoughts turned to survival.

There were days when I looked at my daughter and wondered how I would provide even the basics—food, nappies, shelter. For a brief, terrifying moment, I even considered prostitution. But as soon as the thought formed, I rejected it. I couldn't bear the idea of leaving my daughter with strangers, not after all she had already endured.

Instead, I chose a different path. I decided to offer laundry services, washing clothes for others to earn whatever small income I could—anything that allowed me to keep my baby close and safe.

One neighbour asked me to house-sit while she was away. I agreed, hoping for a change of environment and maybe a small sense of normalcy. But while I stayed in her home, I discovered that someone had broken into my tiny shack.

Fear washed over me.

My first thought was not about what had been taken, but whether my daughter was safe anymore. The break-in only deepened my anxiety. I barely slept, my mind consumed with worry and my heart aching for the security and comfort of my parents' home—something that felt impossibly far away.

As June drew nearer, the reality of my financial struggle grew heavier.

Peter still refused to support our child. The only offer he made was a twisted one: he told me to reconcile with him. The idea of going back to him filled me with dread. Yet my pockets were empty, my child had needs, and options were disappearing.

I had nothing left for nappies. I resorted to using old pieces of cloth for my baby, doing whatever I could to keep her clean and dry. Neighbours noticed and began to gossip. Their whispers and looks stabbed at my dignity, but I had no energy left to defend myself. I learned to ignore their judgmental stares because, at the end of the day, none of them were carrying my burdens.

Hope began to fade.

Little by little, my dreams of a better future seemed to dissolve under the weight of poverty and rejection. Tears became part of my daily routine. But then, a small lifeline appeared.

There was a local organisation called YABANA that provided food for the less fortunate. I swallowed my pride and went there. Their support was small, but it kept us from complete starvation.

At the same time, I searched everywhere for work—but each potential employer looked at my baby and saw a problem, not a person. My child, who gave me purpose, became the reason doors closed in my face.

Still, I refused to surrender to hopelessness completely.

Deep inside, there remained a spark of defiance. I told myself that my current situation did not have the right to define my entire future. I consciously chose to stay strong, to believe that somehow, one day, I would rise above all of this and give my child a better life.

But around me, the atmosphere was growing heavier.

People openly doubted my story about Peter and our daughter. His polished lies and practiced charm worked in his favour. I, on the other hand, was tired, poor, and emotionally shattered— a much easier target to discredit.

Some people started to avoid me completely, as if my truth was contagious.

I felt like a stranger in a place I once knew. I often wondered if staying silent from the beginning would have been less painful. Maybe if I had never reported the abuse, I wouldn't be this isolated. But every time that thought surfaced, I remembered: I spoke up for my child. And that, no matter the cost, was not something I could regret.

Eventually, I accepted that legal justice would not come—not in this broken system, not in this lifetime. For my daughter's privacy and protection, I stopped speaking publicly about what had happened. But silence did not erase the pain.

Inside, the wound remained open.

Peter behaved as though he had won. His smugness, his little provocations, his confidence in the community's support all made my suffering feel worse. I had no job, no stable income, and no way to feed my small family. I was pushed into a painful corner.

In the end, out of sheer survival, I made a decision that broke my own heart: I reconciled with Peter on the surface, while secretly doing everything I could to shield my daughter from further harm.

This choice came with a heavy cost.

Many people in the community concluded that my return to Peter "proved" I had been lying all along. They said I had made up the story about the abuse just to take control of his shop. To them, my survival decision became evidence that I was manipulative, not a mother trying to stay alive with her child.

When I visited Peter's house, the humiliations continued.

His wife moved freely around the home—a home I had sacrificed and worked to help build—while I was treated like an outsider. I sat outside most of the time, sometimes offered scraps of food or pieces of bread, as if I were a beggar at the door.

Back at my shack, things grew worse.

The place became a target for petty thieves. One day, police officers came to question me about a stolen car that had been abandoned nearby. The way they questioned me made it clear they saw my poverty as suspicious, as if being poor made me capable of anything.

I defended myself with every bit of strength I had left. Eventually, they saw in my words and tears that I was innocent, and they relented. Some people from the community, moved by everything I had gone through, pressured Peter to at least rent a small house for me and my child.

He did.

But the new place didn't bring peace.

The other tenants in the complex treated me with the same suspicion and contempt I had already grown used to. Their stares, their whispers, their coldness followed me into this new space. Even the landlord, who should have been neutral, took their side when complaints about me arose.

The rumour that I had lied about the abuse spread further.

People said I had invented the entire story as a way to take over Peter's shop. They didn't see a traumatised mother. They saw a schemer, a liar, an outcast. The more they talked, the more I withdrew.

I retreated into my small rented room.

I went out less and less. The walls became both my prison and my protection. Alone with my thoughts, I cried silently, mourning not just what had been done to us, but also how the

world chose to respond.

I lived with the heartbreak of knowing that truth does not always win in this world.

But even in that room, surrounded by judgment and misunderstanding, a part of me still refused to die—the part that believed that my story was not over, that one day all this pain could become the foundation of something stronger, kinder, and more powerful than anything they could imagine.

19

CHAPTER 19

MOCKERY, COLLAPSE, AND A CRY TO HEAVEN

One afternoon, as I sat outside trying to catch a little warmth from the weak sun, I overheard a group of women talking. At first, I didn't pay attention—until I realised they were speaking about my daughter.

Their words sliced through me.

They mocked my innocent child, saying she already "understood adult things," that she was "on a woman's level." To speak like that about a baby who had already suffered so much was beyond cruel. Their laughter echoed in my chest like knives. In that moment, a fierce, burning desire rose inside me—not just for my own justice, but for my daughter's. She had done nothing to deserve any of this.

As I tried to rebuild my life, I encountered constant disrespect and exploitation.

People saw my need and took advantage of it. They underestimated me, treated me like I had no worth, and used my desperation as an opportunity to demean me. I became "the one you could send," the one who would do the jobs no one else wanted—for almost nothing.

One night, a woman called me, saying she had fought with her husband. She offered me R50 to come to her house, clean up a soiled newspaper with her own waste on it, and lock her door afterward.

I felt humiliated even hearing the request.

But I was also a mother with a hungry child.

Against all my pride and discomfort, I agreed. R50 meant food. R50 meant one more night that my baby wouldn't go to bed hungry. I did what she asked, but inside I felt smaller with every step.

This was not the only time.

People began giving me demeaning tasks, secure in the knowledge that I was too desperate to refuse. The community soon found an ugly nickname for me: "the community washing machine," mocking how I washed clothes and did odd jobs for survival.

Their words landed on me like stones.

Day by day, I felt my dignity eroding. It was as if I was disappearing under the weight of shame and constant struggle.

Then Peter reappeared.

One day he came to see me, his face filled with smug satisfaction. He proudly announced that his wife was pregnant—with twins. Instead of sharing the news with humility, he used it as a weapon, a way to remind me of my place in his story.

Before leaving, he delivered one more cruel blow: he accused me of using witchcraft, of casting spells on his wife.

His baseless accusation said everything about his character, not mine.

After he left, I sat quietly and cried. Not just for what he said, but for everything he represented: selfishness, cruelty, and a complete lack of remorse for the pain he had caused.

Around us, injustice seemed to reign.

Some people with power and money behaved as if they could do anything without consequences. They defended their own wrongs while trampling on truth and humanity. To them, I was weak, broken, and defeated—someone easy to ignore, easy to blame.

But they were wrong about one thing.

They didn't know that, in my quiet suffering, I was observing, remembering, recording every injustice in my heart. Every cruel word. Every mockery. Every act of betrayal. They thought I was too damaged to ever rise, too broken to ever speak.

One conversation, in particular, burned itself into my memory.

There was a man who often came to see Peter. He would openly ask Peter to buy him alcohol, never once acknowledging the pain I was going through. One day I overheard him say, "You know I helped you, so you must buy me a drink." His words

were dripping with entitlement.

Hearing this, while I was still crying out for justice and being ignored, left a bitter taste in my mouth. Here was a man proudly reminding Peter of how he had "helped" him, while my cries, my daughter's suffering, and the truth meant nothing.

Sometimes it felt like my pain entertained people.

But there were rare exceptions.

One woman in the community treated me with genuine kindness. She lived nearby and became a quiet friend. I had done some jobs for her, and from there, a small bond of trust formed. Her kindness shone against the darkness of everyone else's cruelty.

One evening, she asked me for a favour. She wanted me to fetch her boyfriend from the nearby shops while she tidied up her home. I agreed and went with my baby to bring him.

On our way back, we met Peter.

He called my name sharply. I felt obligated to respond, so I quickly explained to my friend's boyfriend what was happening and assumed he would continue the short distance to her house. Peter's reaction was immediate and angry.

He demanded to know who the man was. I calmly explained that he was my friend's boyfriend and that I was simply doing her a favour. But Peter's focus shifted. He began scolding and insulting me for being out late with the baby, twisting an innocent situation into something suspicious.

His words were harsh, full of possessiveness and accusations.

The memory of what happened next is hazy.

The next thing I remember is waking up in my friend's small room. My clothes were damp, my body freezing, my throat tight, and my baby crying next to me. I tried to speak, but my voice felt stuck.

My friend explained what had happened.

After I dropped off her boyfriend, she saw Peter leaving the yard on his bicycle. When she asked where I was, he ignored her and rode away. A short while later, she heard my baby crying outside. She went to check and found me collapsed on the ground, unresponsive.

With her boyfriend's help, they carried me into her room and tried everything to revive me. After some time, my body finally responded. I started breathing again. It dawned on me with a cold shock: I had fainted. The trauma, stress, and exhaustion had finally crashed down on me physically.

One question haunted me:

Why did Peter just leave?

He saw my condition. He knew I was vulnerable. Yet he walked—or rather, rode—away, leaving me there in the dark with our baby. That kind of coldness is something you don't forget.

The next morning brought more pain.

I learned that some people in the community had seen what happened—and laughed. Some even praised Peter, calling him "a hero" for how he handled me. Others admitted to witnessing the whole incident but did nothing. They watched a mother collapse and chose silence.

Among those who failed me were people who wore uniforms and titles: police officers, health workers, and Christians— people who should have embodied protection, care, and compassion. Their inaction spoke loudly.

One day, the landlord—who had once invited us to watch TV as if he cared—suddenly pretended to be concerned about me. But I knew better. I knew he had helped bury my daughter's abuse case. His loyalty was clearly with Peter and the popular narrative, not with truth.

I confronted him.

I asked him why he supported Peter instead of justice. Why he stood with a man who had harmed a child rather than with the victim. My questions stripped away his fake kindness.

He snapped.

He ordered me out of his house immediately, his concern turning into visible rage. Before I could move, he took my daughter out of the house and

Ordered me to follow her. Panic rushed through my body. I tried to calm things down, apologising but he ignored me.

His anger escalated further. He began throwing stones at me.

The humiliation was complete.

As if on cue, Peter arrived. Instead of defending me or calming the situation, he took the landlord's side without hesitation. He showed no concern for what was happening to me or our child. He simply said that if I didn't have a place to stay, I should sort it out myself—that he had his wife and family to think about.

At that moment, I felt the full weight of abandonment.

The community's laughter, their judgment, their cruel words— all of it pressed on my chest, making it hard to breathe. I had no one. No family nearby. No ally. No safe place to fall apart.

I stood there with my heart shattered, and there was only one place left to turn.

Inside, I cried out to God:

“Why me, God? Why is this my life?”

The cruelest part of all of this wasn’t just what people did—it was how quickly they judged without ever knowing the full story. They formed their opinions based on rumours and lies, never once bothering to ask what I had truly survived.

Yet even in that crushing loneliness, a part of me refused to disappear.

The part that still knew my truth.
The part that still believed, somehow, someday, God would answer that desperate question—not with words, but with a new chapter.

20

CHAPTER 20

THE ILLUSION OF HELP: WHEN "RESCUE" IS ANOTHER TRAP

Desperation had become my shadow. It followed me everywhere—into every room, every decision, every sleepless night. It made me vulnerable, not just to hunger and hardship, but to people who wore kindness like a mask.

Trust became a luxury I could no longer afford.

I then met a woman named Miss Loveness. She presented herself as a caring, supportive friend—someone who understood my struggle and wanted to help.

Part of me remained cautious. I had seen too much, trusted too many, and been betrayed more times than I could count. Still, another part of me was exhausted and desperate for a safe place. Moving in with her felt, at that moment, like the only real option—a small chance to breathe.

But, as so many times before, hope didn't last long.

Barely a week had passed when Miss Loveness invited Peter into her home.

I was shocked.

In our conversations, I had confided in her—shared pieces of my story, my pain, my fears. But instead of protecting that trust, she handed it over to him like gossip. She questioned him openly, repeating private details I had told her in confidence.

Peter did what he always did best: he performed.

With his well-practised lies, his calm tone, and his defensive charm, he slowly turned the situation upside down. He painted me as the problem—exaggerating, lying, manipulating. By the end of their talk, Miss Loveness had shifted from sympathy to suspicion.

Her words began to echo his.

The woman who had initially shown concern now repeated his accusations, doubting my story and subtly blaming me. It was a familiar pain—being betrayed and then made to feel like the villain.

But this time, I wasn't completely broken by it.

The resilience I had built through countless betrayals stood up to shield me. I recognised what was happening. I saw clearly that I had to protect myself and, above all, my child. Whatever "kindness" she had shown me was conditional, fragile, and easily blown away by Peter's lies.

In that clarity, her real motives surfaced.

Eventually, Miss Loveness dropped the act.

She admitted that she had not taken me in simply out of kindness. Her real plan was to send me to stay with her children in another community so I could look after them—unpaid, unprotected, and unconsulted. My presence in her house had never been about helping me; it was about using me.

The next day, she arranged a taxi to take me to this new place.

I didn't know exactly where I was going. The driver, too, seemed unsure of the location. As the hours passed and the sun began to set, my anxiety grew. I held my baby closer, fear gnawing at me. Being lost in an unfamiliar place, with a small child and no control over where we were headed, was terrifying.

As darkness approached, the driver finally managed to reach Miss Loveness home.

Following her vague directions, he dropped me off at a gated property. I thanked him sincerely—he had tried his best to get us there safely.

But once I stepped inside, reality hit me hard.

The house was in chaos. Dirty dishes were stacked high, papers and clutter covered the tables, and dust lay thick on everything. There was no welcome. No prepared space for me and my child. No bed. No clean water to drink.

The air was heavy with neglect.

I realised very quickly what this place was: not a refuge, but a workplace. I had not been brought here as a guest to be helped, but as unpaid labour expected to clean, care, and manage a mess I didn't create—without even the basics for my own dignity.

The dust triggered my sinus problems. Breathing was hard, sleeping was harder. And the message was clear: I wasn't there to be supported. I was there to serve.

Before I left her former home, I begged Miss Loveness one thing.

I told her, clearly and earnestly, not to tell Peter where I was going. I needed distance from him. I needed space to think, heal, and protect my daughter. She had promised me she wouldn't share my location.

I badly wanted to believe her.

But as I lay there that night, surrounded by disorder and

breathing in dust, unease settled in my chest like a stone. Something felt wrong. It was the familiar tug of my instincts, warning me that the danger wasn't over yet.

The next day, my fear was confirmed.

Peter showed up at the house.

He arrived casually, as if he had every right to be there. When I asked how he found the place, he said calmly that Miss Loveness had given him the directions.

Her betrayal cut me deeply.

After everything I had survived. After all the times I had been silenced, blamed, and exposed. After asking so clearly for just one boundary—she had broken it as if my safety meant nothing. She had chosen him over my protection.

In that moment, I felt my heart harden in a new way. It wasn't that I stopped feeling pain—it was that I stopped being surprised by it from certain types of people. Desperation had led me straight into yet another trap. And now I knew, more clearly than ever:

Even when I was at my lowest, I could not afford to switch off my vigilance.

Even when I needed help, I had to question the motives behind it.

Even in the name of "friendship," people could still expose me to the very danger I was running from.

But this time, the difference was this:

I saw it.

I recognised it.

And I knew I had to find a way to stand on my own—truly on my own—if I ever wanted real safety for myself and my daughter.

21

CHAPTER 21

TRAPPED BY SELF-INTEREST: WHEN "HELP" HAS A PRICE

Soon, Miss Loveness's true intentions became impossible to ignore.

She began pressuring me to reconcile with Peter—but not out of any concern for my emotional well-being or my daughter's safety. Her interest was financial. In her eyes, getting back with him meant access to money that could benefit not only me, but her and her children too.

She shamelessly encouraged me to sleep with him, speaking as if it were a smart strategy rather than a painful return to a man who had deeply wounded me. It was as if my trauma, my scars, and my daughter's suffering meant nothing compared to what she hoped to gain.

Desperate for some kind of stability, I reluctantly gave in.

I was tired. Tired of hunger. Tired of uncertainty. Tired of feeling like every path led to another dead end. So I tried to convince myself that maybe, just maybe, this arrangement could at least bring some financial relief.

But soon, the truth surfaced.

I discovered that Miss Loveness was secretly working with Peter behind my back. She spoke to him in private, sharing things about me, and even worse, she was collecting money from him directly. The illusion of sisterhood shattered.

Her own children, without realising it, exposed everything through their careless bragging. They spoke about the money and arrangements as if it were a normal thing, revealing just how vulnerable I had become—reduced to a topic in their household transactions.

The full weight of my exploitation began to show.

Day after day, I carried the entire burden of the household.

I cleaned the house from top to bottom. I worked in the garden under the blazing sun. I looked after her children, who were lazy, disobedient, and often rude. Their behaviour was wild and disrespectful, but instead of correcting them, Miss Loveness stayed silent, watching as they spoke to me however they pleased.

I was treated like a live-in servant, not a guest. I was working constantly, yet I held no power, no voice, no recognition.

Then another disturbing truth emerged.

It became clear that both Miss Loveness and her husband were failing their children in a basic way: financially. They had jobs, but their kids' needs were often not met. In that vacuum, Peter stepped in.

He started providing for their children.

On the surface, it looked like generosity. But in my heart, I sensed something more sinister. I couldn't stop wondering: was he paying them in the same way he expected to "support" me—through manipulation and sexual favors? Was this just another web of exploitation that we were all caught in?

If Peter hadn't stepped in, the children and I would have gone hungry for many days. But unlike them, I had no one else to call, no friends to lean on, no family nearby. I was alone.

One memory still stands out sharply.

Miss Loveness once gave her son money, clearly instructing him to buy essential groceries for the house.

When he returned, he brought back a tube of Colgate, a few carrots, and a brand-new speaker for himself.

His own desires took priority over the family's basic needs.

When I told Miss Loveness what he had done, her solution was not to correct him—it was to silence me. She told me to lie to her husband and pretend everything was fine so that he

wouldn't beat their son.

Once again, I was pulled into a web of deception, forced to protect a dysfunctional system that was already breaking everyone inside it.

The signs of neglect were everywhere.

There were days when the children didn't even have lotion for school, their skin dry and uncared for, another small but painful sign of parental neglect. My heart wouldn't let me ignore it.

So I got creative.

I melted candle wax, mixed it with used cooking oil, and added a bit of my own roll-on just to create a makeshift lotion for them. It was a poor solution, but it showed how desperately I was trying to care for children who were not even mine—while their own parents treated me like I was less than human.

Yet, even my daughter was not spared from cruelty.

One day, Miss Loveness's children asked to take my daughter out to play. Something inside me resisted. I hesitated, worried about how she might be treated, but I also wanted her to experience a bit of normal childhood. Eventually, I agreed, hoping they would be kind.

CHAPTER21

They came back with her in tears.

Her little face was wet with crying, and I could see distress written all over her. I asked what happened, and I learned that one of the other children—a friend of theirs—had thrown an insect at her while insulting her, calling her ugly and unwanted. Those words broke me.

My daughter, who had already faced so much before she could even understand it, was now being attacked and humiliated by other children.

I told Miss Loveness what had happened.

Her response was not what a mother, or any caring adult, should give. She brushed it off, reacting with doubt and distance. She even went so far as to suggest that maybe her own daughter had been involved somehow, as if that deflected responsibility. There was no apology. No correction. No comfort for my child. Once again, the message was clear: our pain did not matter.

I was carrying the house. I was raising children that weren't mine. I was being used as a bridge between Peter and their needs. And still, my daughter and I were treated as if we were nothing.

But deep inside, something in me was shifting.

I was no longer just hurt—I was becoming quietly, powerfully determined. I could see now, more than ever, that I would never find real safety or dignity in places built on lies, selfishness, and exploitation.

And slowly, the idea began to grow:

One day, I would leave all of this behind—for good.
I would find a way to stand on my own two feet.
And I would raise my daughter in a world where she knew her worth.

22

CHAPTER 22

DEATH AT THE DOOR AND DEEPENING TRAPS

One night, sleep brought no rest—only terror.

I had a vivid, haunting dream. A man dressed in black, his face hidden behind a cream-white mask smeared with blood, appeared in the darkness. In eerie silence, he carried my daughter in his arms. He walked over and gently laid her down in her usual sleeping place, then disappeared into the shadows
without a word.

I woke up with my heart pounding.

A cold, chilling fear gripped me. It didn't feel like just a dream; it felt like a warning. I rushed to check on my daughter.

What I found froze my blood.

She was lying still. Too still. Her small body was cold to the touch. She wasn't moving. She wasn't responding. For a terrifying moment, she looked lifeless.

Panic exploded inside me.

I screamed for help and woke everyone in the house. They stumbled into the room, their confusion quickly turning to fear. The scene felt unreal, like I was watching a horror movie with no way to stop it.

Desperate, my mind grabbed onto the memory of some holy water I had kept in the house. I wasn't even sure how strong my faith was at that moment, but I had nothing else—no money, no car, no medical help nearby. Just that water and my desperate hope.

With shaking hands, I sprinkled the holy water over her small, cold body.

For a moment, nothing happened.

Then slowly, gently, she stirred.

A faint movement. A shallow breath. Then another.

She was weak and initially paralysed; her little limbs wouldn't move properly. But life had returned. Bit by bit, painfully slowly, she began to come back to herself. I watched her with a mixture of relief and terror, knowing just how close I had come to losing her.

I didn't sleep after that.

The image of her lying there, motionless and cold, refused to leave my mind. I kept replaying everything— the dream, the moment I found her, the way she came back. I tried to make sense of it, but nothing could explain it fully.

When Miss Loveness finally returned, I told her what had happened.

I expected concern. Shock. Some kind of comfort.

Instead, her reaction was indifferent. Cold. As if I were describing something small and forgettable. Her lack of emotion cut me deeply. It was as if my fear, my child's brush with death, meant absolutely nothing to her.

Barely a week later, she left again.

This time, she didn't even pretend to care. She gathered her children and walked out, leaving me alone in the house with my still-recovering daughter. No food. No support. No explanation.

Just abandonment.

That memory still stings—the sight of her walking away, leaving me and my child behind as if we were a problem she could simply step over.

From then on, I lived in constant vigilance.

I watched my daughter as she slept, terrified of what might happen if I let my guard down. I barely rested. My fear was a prison, and every breath she took was something I guarded with everything in me.

One day, her husband returned home.

The atmosphere in the house shifted immediately. He wasted no time in assigning me chores. He ordered me to clean a pile of heavily soiled pots, the grime thick and stubborn, as if it had been building up for a long time.

I was already exhausted to my bones.

Still, I spent the entire day scrubbing, my fingers sore, my hands raw, my back aching. When I was finally done, he inspected the pots.

Instead of appreciation, he accused me.

He claimed the pots had not been that dirty before, implying that I must have neglected my duties, that I was somehow at fault. His words added another layer of unfair blame to a life already overloaded with it.

I felt like I could not win.

On top of that, I was made responsible for caring for a sixyear-old boy in the house who suffered from incontinence. It became my job to wash him, clean up after his accidents, and scrub his soiled clothes—on top of the housework, the cooking, the garden, and caring for my own child.

I wasn't a guest.
I wasn't a friend.
I was their servant.

It became painfully clear: they hadn't taken me in to help me. They wanted a free maid, a desperate woman they could overwork and control.

One day, after working in the garden under the harsh sun, the whole family gathered and started issuing orders like I was an employee on call.

Clean the whole house.
Prepare a big meal.
Do this. Do that.

The list seemed endless.

By the end of the day, my body was beyond tired. I felt like I was fading. My emotions, my energy, my sense of self—all worn thin.

Then, a small sliver of hope appeared.

I managed to get a four-day job around Christmas. It wasn't much, but to me, it felt like a miracle—a chance to earn some money and maybe give my daughter a slightly better holiday, or at least a meal that didn't come from desperation.

I left my daughter in their care.

Every step I took away from her that first day felt heavy. But I had to work. I had to try. I poured all my strength into the job, focusing on the thought of bringing something back for her.

When I returned, joy was the last thing I felt.

I found my daughter unwell. There was a swollen lump forming under her small armpit. My heart dropped. Fear crashed over me. After everything she had already endured, seeing her in pain again tore me apart.

Then came another blow.

Miss Loveness confessed that she had contacted Peter while I was away—despite my repeated, urgent warnings about him, despite everything he had done.

A child's innocence does not remove the impact of their choices.

She had reached out to a man I was trying to protect my daughter from. Her desire for connection, or perhaps curiosity, had overshadowed the danger I had tried so hard to explain.

It felt like a deep, sharp stab—a betrayal from within the only "home" I had, even if that home was already broken.

By then, the children's disrespect had reached boiling point. Their attitudes were uglier. Their words sharper. Their lack of respect for me, and even for my daughter, became unbearable. And this time, my patience broke.

I could no longer swallow the insults, hide the pain, or pretend to be okay. All the fear, exhaustion, humiliation, and betrayal I had buried inside climbed to the surface.

Something had to change.

Whether it was my surroundings, my decisions, or the people in my life—this chapter was clearly becoming too dangerous to continue.

My heart was shattered.
My trust was gone.
But somewhere under all that pain, a quiet voice was growing louder:

You cannot stay here.

You cannot keep sacrificing yourself and your daughter like this.

You deserve more. She deserves more.

23

CHAPTER 23

EVICTED, ISOLATED, BUT NOT DESTROYED

The tension in the house had been building for a long time.

After the confrontation with the children, their parents overheard only the end of our exchange. Without asking what really happened or trying to understand the deeper issues, they did what so many adults in my life had done—they chose their own children's version of events and turned on me.

They ordered me to leave.

That night, I lay on the hard floor, turning from side to side, unable to find rest. Sleep offered no escape. My mind raced with questions: Where would I go? What would happen to my daughter? How much more could I take?

CHAPTER23

Morning came far too quickly.

As the first light crept through the cracks in the walls, they added another layer of humiliation: they called Peter. His presence wasn't about concern—it was a show, a final act of public rejection.

I was pushed to leave, tears streaming down my face, trying desperately to hold on to a shred of dignity as I carried my sick child and my few belongings out of their yard.

By then, Miss Loveness's intentions were painfully clear.

She had never truly cared about me or my daughter. She had seen our desperation as an opportunity. A chance to benefit, to gain access to Peter's money, to secure free labour and constant service.

Early on, there had been a moment that my spirit recognized as a warning.

She had once insisted that I leave my baby in her care.

Something inside me screamed no. My instincts rose up in protest. I refused, telling her clearly that I alone would care for my child. Later, she went even further.

She instructed Peter to take my baby. That was the final confirmation of what I had already suspected: there was nothing protective or loving in her intentions. Her only concern was what she could get out of this situation. We

were never guests in her home—we were investments, tools, bargaining chips.

At that point, I had reached my breaking point.

Leaving—no matter how painful, how humiliating—was better than staying one more day in that trap. In a twisted way, their act of throwing me out made the decision for me. They closed a door I might have struggled to shut on my own.

But they weren't done yet.

Before I left, they asked me where I planned to go. The question sounded concerned, but their eyes told the truth—it wasn't matter. It was a calculation.

I mentioned a woman named Miss Louis, someone I had met during my pregnancy. My uncle had introduced her as his "sister," though the exact nature of their relationship was never fully clear. Still, in my mind, she represented a possible place of refuge.

Miss Loveness and her husband knew her well.

In a cold, deliberate move, they decided to call her husband. They placed the phone on speaker, making sure I could hear every word.

They asked if he knew me.

He said yes.

That's when the lies began.

They told him I had been abusive to their children. They painted themselves as righteous and justified in kicking me out. I stood there listening, tears pouring down my face, unable to defend myself, my voice buried under their accusations.

On the other end of the line, Miss Louis's husband hardened.

He said he would not allow me to stay with them. He pointed out that I wasn't even blood-related, and that my uncle had a history of "forcing relationships" with his family. Then, with cruel finality, he declared that they didn't want anyone who
was "abusive to children" in their home.

The bitter irony cut deep.

My daughter, an innocent child, had been the real victim of abuse. I had been the one fighting for her, suffering for her, losing everything for her. Yet here I was being branded as a danger to children.

When the call ended, I had nowhere to go.

No plan. No refuge. Just humiliation and despair.

They threw my new backpack onto the ground—a small thing I had managed to buy as a symbol of starting over. My daughter's new shoes, which I had saved so hard to afford, followed. To them, these were the only things that "belonged" to me.

Everything else, including my dignity, felt like it had been

stripped away.

I gathered my few remaining clothes mechanically, my movements numb.

Neighbours stood at their gates, watching. Some with curiosity, some with judgment, some with a mix of both. Their eyes felt like arrows. I wished the ground would open and swallow me. In the middle of all that humiliation, one person saw me.

A woman from the community, who had quietly admired my strength and perseverance, stepped forward. She saw the injustice of what was happening. Moved by compassion, she offered to take me in, to give me a place to stay.

But kindness hit a wall of hate.

Loveness and her husband refused her offer immediately. They said, in front of everyone, that they didn't want me anywhere near their community. No reasons, no explanation—just pure rejection.

Their only justification was simple and cruel:
"We just don't want her."

With no other options, I had no choice but to walk away.

I turned to Peter, pushing my pride down as far as I could, and asked him for one simple favour: help me carry my luggage to the bus stop. Not as a father, not as a partner, just as one human being to another.

He refused.

He said he had a bus to catch. As if a schedule mattered more than a struggling woman and his own sick child.

Desperate, I turned to some children passing by and asked for their help. Their faces showed sympathy, but fear quickly overshadowed it. They had been warned not to help me and
were afraid of the consequences if they disobeyed.

So even they stepped back.

I was left to carry my burdens alone—physically, emotionally, and spiritually.

But as I stood there, something else quietly rose inside me.

I realised that, once again, I had survived what was designed to break me.

I had been evicted, slandered, and rejected.

Yet I was still standing. My daughter was still in my arms. My story was still being written.

They had taken my shelter, my reputation, and my sense of belonging.

What they could not take was my will to keep going.

24

CHAPTER 24

CAST OUT, YET CARRIED

They didn't just throw me out—they escorted me out.

In a final act of petty cruelty, Miss Loveness and her family walked with me to the bus stop. It wasn't supported; it was a mocking parade. As I climbed into the crowded taxi, their voices rose behind me, loud enough for everyone to hear:

"Go, go, we don't want you here. See what you'll do and where you'll go."

Their words chased me into the vehicle like stones.

The other passengers stared—some with curiosity, others with discomfort. No one said anything, but their eyes felt heavy on my skin. I held my daughter close and, for the first time in that long, humiliating day, I couldn't hold it in anymore.

Tears slipped down my cheeks, silent but unstoppable.

I had no clear destination. No safe place waiting. Just a taxi moving forward while my life felt stuck in place.

As evening approached, the taxi finally stopped and dropped me off in an area I didn't recognize.

The sky was painted with fading shades of orange and grey as the sun sank. The road was unfamiliar. The air felt colder. Fear crept up my spine.

I stepped down with my baby in my arms and my small pieces of luggage beside me. When the taxi pulled away, its dust settled around us like a curtain closing on that brutal chapter.

I was alone.

Exhausted. Afraid. Overwhelmed.

My daughter coughed softly, each cough stabbing my heart. She felt feverish in my arms, her tiny body too warm, too fragile. I had no nappies for her. No proper food. No bed. No plan.

The bags I carried felt impossibly heavy—not just with clothes, but with the weight of everything I had lost. I hadn't bathed properly. My clothes held the smell of days of hard work, stress, and pain. My body wanted to collapse, but my reality wouldn't

let me.

I stood there on that dusty roadside and cried.

Not a quiet, hidden cry—but a broken one. A cry born from too many closed doors and too much injustice.

In that moment of absolute helplessness, there was only one thing left for me to do: pray.

I didn't have fancy words. Just a desperate, silent plea from a shattered heart:

"God, please. Do something. Help me. Show me You're still here."

As darkness crept closer, swallowing the colours of the sky, an unexpected figure appeared.

A vehicle slowed down and pulled over. The driver recognised me. He was one of the few faces in the community that hadn't turned away from me.

He saw me—really saw me.

He asked what had happened. My words came in broken waves, spilling out all the pain, all the rejection, all the injustice. He listened, his face full of concern, not judgment.

Then he did something small but powerful: he offered me shelter for the night.

Just one night. But that one night meant everything.

I went with him, holding my baby as if she were my last piece of sanity. The home was not a palace, but to me it felt like a refuge—a place where, for a few hours at least, I wasn't being screamed at, accused, or thrown out.

The next day, he decided to confront the situation.

He went to see Miss Loveness and her husband, hoping to understand why they had treated me so cruelly. Maybe, in his hope, he believed that reasoning with them could soften their hearts or at least bring some truth to the surface.

When he came back, his face told the story before he spoke.

Their response had been vicious.

They had told him to throw me out and to never help me again. They warned him that if I died while staying at his place, he would "face serious consequences." Instead of admitting their wrongdoing, they doubled down on their hatred.

Even when I was gone from their house, they still wanted control over my fate.

But his visit brought me something precious: clarity.

It proved, once again, that I couldn't rely on them, or people like them, for justice, compassion, or fairness. Their goal was not just to be rid of me—they wanted to make sure no one else

helped me either.

In that moment, a hard but necessary truth became clear:

If I wanted even the smallest chance at justice, I had to speak for myself.

I decided I needed to go to Miss Louis—the woman whose husband had already refused me over the phone, based on their lies. She hadn't heard my side. She only knew their story. And as long as that remained the only version, I would stay condemned in their eyes.

The good Samaritan agreed to help me one more time.

He offered to escort me to her place. It was not a guaranteed solution, but it was a chance—a slim one, but still a chance—to tell my truth.

As we travelled, my emotions swirled.

Fear. Hope. Anger. Exhaustion.

Would she listen? Would she slam the door in my face? Had her heart already been poisoned beyond repair by their venomous

words? I didn't know.

But I knew this:

I couldn't keep running without trying to clear my name.
I couldn't keep carrying the weight of their lies in silence.

And I couldn't stop fighting—not while my daughter needed me.

So, tired but determined, I kept going.

One more house.
One more door.
One more chance to be heard.

25

CHAPTER 25

THE DECEPTIVE SAVIOUR: WHEN "HELP" HIDES HARM

On the surface, Miss Louis looked like everything I thought I needed.

She appeared deeply religious, always talking about God, blessings, and righteousness. In my desperation, she seemed like a lifeline—someone rooted in faith who might finally offer stable, genuine help.

But beneath her polished image lived something very different.

Her heart was steeped in gossip and a hunger for control. She loved to talk about other people, to dissect their lives, to plant seeds of conflict where there had once been peace. Her words were sharp, often leaving invisible wounds behind.

She carried herself as if goodness belonged to her alone.

She truly believed she was above others, that kindness, morality, and “good deeds” were her personal territory. Everyone else, in her eyes, fell short. She needed others to acknowledge her superiority and to see her as uniquely blessed and chosen.

People had warned me about her.

They told me she caused fights. That she twisted stories. That she enjoyed stirring trouble and then standing back, playing innocent while others clashed. But at the time, I dismissed these warnings as jealousy or judgment. I needed help, and I wanted to believe she really was the kind, generous woman she presented to the world.

I would later regret that deeply.

Behind her religious words, she was a master manipulator.

She had perfected the art of appearing holy while secretly fuelling divisions. She spread lies as if they were truth, carefully crafted to make others look desperate or dangerous while she remained the “good person” in the story.

What made it worse was her complete denial.

Even when confronted with proof of what she had done, she would twist events, deny responsibility, and claim she was only trying to help. She wore the label "good person" proudly, while her actions exposed a cruel delight in using people's pain and secrets against them.

Being around her required extreme caution.

I quickly learned that anything said in her presence could—and would—be repeated elsewhere, often changed, exaggerated, or taken out of context. Her questions weren't innocent; they were calculated, designed to dig out personal information she could later weaponise.

She interrogated in the name of concern, but her curiosity had sharp teeth.

If I had understood her true nature from the beginning, I would have kept my distance. But by the time I saw clearly, I was already entangled in her web.

Her control ran deep.

If you tried to correct her or speak the truth, she didn't stop. She simply created a new version of reality where she was the victim, and you were the problem. It was like arguing with someone who lived in their own world, where facts didn't matter—only the story that made her look better.

Sometimes I found myself wondering:

Would she understand pain and humility only if her own children were treated the way she treated others? Would empathy finally reach her then?

At first, I believed her when she said people were "jealous" of her.

She talked about others as if they were always attacking her, misunderstanding her, or trying to bring her down. I felt sorry for her. I thought, "Maybe she really has suffered. Maybe her kindness has been abused."

She looked blessed from the outside—stable home, respect, a position in the community. I hoped, naively, that some of that blessing might overflow into my life too.

But the pattern was always the same.

She built people up with words, then tore them down behind their backs. She extended "help" with one hand while holding a knife of gossip in the other.

Eventually, my turn came.

When I finally swallowed my pride and asked for her help, she arranged for me to stay at the home of a woman named Miss Mclony. This woman needed someone to look after her house while she was away for a while.

There was even a small payment attached—R800.

To someone in my position, that amount felt like gold. It was hope. It could mean food, nappies, maybe a little stability. I accepted the arrangement with gratitude, not knowing I was walking straight into another kind of trap.

I stayed at Miss Mclony's place for three weeks.

I took care of the house faithfully. But after a while, hunger began to bite. There was no food coming in, and I had no money. Pride battled with need, but eventually, I had to act.

I went back to Miss Louis and asked for R50.

A small amount, but to me, it meant survival. I promised her I would pay her back as soon as Miss Mclony returned and gave me the agreed R800.

She gave me the money—but her eyes were sharp, full of nosy curiosity.

"What are you going to do with it?" she asked.

Her question wasn't caring—it was probing. I didn't want to tell her. I just said I needed to take care of "something important." But she didn't let it go.

Day after day, she kept asking.

Her questions grew more insistent, more invasive. She wanted details. She wanted to know exactly what I planned to buy.

Finally, worn down by her persistence, I told the truth.

I said I needed mealie-meal—basic food. Just something to eat. Something to keep me and my child from going to bed hungry.

If I had known what she would do with that information, I would have kept silent.

When the end of the month came and Miss McClony returned, her attitude toward me had changed.

She was distant. Colder. Guarded. I felt it immediately. I searched my mind, wondering what I had done wrong. I had taken care of her house. I had respected her space. I had waited patiently for her return.

Then the truth came out.

Miss Louis had done it.

She told her that I had come to her "crying for help," claiming that Miss Mclony had abandoned me without food or support, leaving me destitute. She painted me as desperate, manipulative, and ungrateful.

Her story twisted my genuine struggle for survival into a false accusation against the very person giving me shelter.

I was stunned.

I carefully explained the real story to Miss Mclony: that I had simply asked for a small loan, that I had never said she left me with nothing, that my intention was to buy food quietly and pay it back as soon as I could.

I could see confusion in her eyes—caught between the lies she had heard and the truth I was trying to tell.

The damage, however, had already been done.

Trust had been cracked. And once trust is broken, it rarely returns to what it was.

After that, I grew quieter.

I moved through the days with a heavy heart, watching the fragile roof of temporary safety above me start to shake again. I knew what was coming. I felt it.

Another move.
Another loss.
Another unstable ending.

In the silence of those days, a weary question kept echoing inside me:

When will I find a real home?
A place where no one uses me, lies about me, or throws me out?
A place where my daughter and I can finally rest?

What Miss Louis did made one thing painfully clear:

This stay at Miss Mclony's was not going to last.
And once again, I would be back on the road, searching for somewhere—anywhere—to truly belong.

CHAPTER 26

WHEN STABILITY COMES WITH HIDDEN CRUELTY

At Miss Mclony's house, I tried with everything in me to break the pattern.

I wanted, more than anything, to finally find a place where my daughter and I could stay without being thrown out, lied about, or used. So I gave that house my all.

I was respectful in every way. I anticipated her needs and responded quickly whenever she called. I cleaned, cooked, and did whatever was asked of me, constantly aware of how fragile my place there was. Every day, I worked not just with my hands, but with the quiet hope that this time things might be different.

But slowly, month after month, something shifted.

Despite my efforts, Miss McClony grew harsher. Her tone became sharper. Her patience with me is thinner. I tried harder each time, thinking maybe I just wasn't doing enough.

Then I noticed a pattern.

Whenever she came back after visiting Miss Louis, her attitude toward me changed. She would leave the house one way— polite, sometimes even kind—and return distant, cold, and easily irritated with me.

It felt as if my name travelled to her ears before I ever had a chance to defend myself.

Meanwhile, another disturbing pattern was emerging—this time with my daughter.

Whenever certain family members visited, my usually happy, playful little girl became quiet and withdrawn. She seemed sad, her energy dimmed. I also noticed she kept leaving her tea untouched—which was unusual for her.

One day, my concern grew too strong to ignore.

I asked one of the children, calmly, who had made my daughter's tea. The child casually admitted that she had—and added, without a flicker of remorse, that she hadn't put any sugar in it because she "thought" my daughter didn't like sugar.

It was such a small thing on the surface—just sugar. But the intent behind it felt anything but small.

It was calculated. Petty. Cruel.

That moment opened my eyes wider. I started watching more closely.

The very next morning, they prepared Weet-Bix for breakfast. Everyone else received proper bowls of cereal with milk and sugar. When I checked my daughter's bowl, my heart sank.

It looked watery.

It was as if there was no cereal, no milk, no sugar, just a bowl of watery liquid passed off as "breakfast" for my child.

The message was loud and clear.

They were targeting the most vulnerable person in the house— my three-year-old daughter. They couldn't stand me, so they hurt her in the quietest, most cowardly ways.

A wave of protective anger rose inside me.

I went to the kitchen, prepared a proper meal for her, and from that moment I made a firm decision: no one else would prepare her food again. If they wanted to punish me, they would not do it through my child.

But the cruelty didn't stop at starvation games.

One day, a neighbour came to me, her voice full of concern. She told me that the other children had been beating my daughter during playtime.

My heart dropped.

I rushed to the area where they were supposed to be playing. What I saw made my blood run cold.

My little girl—just three years old—was on the ground, covered in sand. Another girl, her own age, was actively hitting her,

while older girls stood around watching and laughing, as if my child's pain was entertainment.

I ran to her, scooped her up into my arms, and held her close. She was shaking, confused, and scared. I took her back home, my mind spinning with anger, grief, and fear.

But the horror didn't end there.

On our way home, another neighbour stopped me. She asked gently why I was sending my daughter to the shop to buy Simba chips for 20 cents.

I froze.

I had never sent my daughter to buy anything. She was far too young to run errands alone.

My stomach twisted as the truth slowly came out.

CHAPTER26

The older girls had been sending my daughter to the shop with just 20 cents—knowing very well it wasn't enough to buy anything. Likely, they were doing it as a cruel joke or a way to embarrass and control her. They used her innocence and obedience for their own entertainment.

I went straight to the shop owner to confirm.

He sighed sadly and told me yes, my daughter had come to his shop three times with that same small coin in her hand, tears on her face, trying to buy chips with money that could never be enough.

It broke my heart.

My child was being used, mocked, and set up to fail by children much older than her.

I did what any mother would do: I spoke up.

I went to Miss McClony and explained everything—the unsweetened tea, the watery Weet-Bix, the beatings during playtime, the shop incident. I told her clearly that my daughter was only three, while the girls involved were ten and older. This wasn't an innocent play. It was bullying. It was abuse.

Her response crushed me.

She dismissed it all as "just children playing."

There was no concern. No anger at the older girls. No protection for my daughter. Instead, her anger turned on me when I said that my daughter would no longer be playing with them.

To her, I was the problem—for trying to protect my child.

As if that wasn't enough, I was then sent to Miss Louis, while Miss McClony followed. Instead of offering understanding, she scolded me for "interfering with the children's play," fully supporting the very behaviour that was harming my daughter.

In that moment, it became painfully clear:

To them, my child's pain was an inconvenience.
My boundaries were disrespectful.

And my attempts to protect her were treated as a crime.

But inside me, a line had been drawn.

I might have had to stay quiet to survive in many situations, but when it came to my daughter's safety, my silence had limits.

I didn't know where we would go next.
I didn't know when this pattern of betrayal and eviction would end.
But I knew this:

I would not let anyone break her spirit without a fight—even if that fight cost me yet another place to live.

27

CHAPTER 27

A CHILD'S TRAUMA AND A MOTHER STRETCHED TO BREAKING**

The cruelty my daughter endured left marks far deeper than anyone around us cared to see.

From that day on, she refused to play with the other children. The laughter, which once drew her in, now scared her. If I tried to step away, even for a moment, she would cling to me and sob, following me everywhere like a little shadow.

To her, those children were no longer playmates. They had become monsters.

We often sought refuge under the shade of a big tree. There, away from the noise, I would sit quietly with her, holding her close, trying to breathe through my own anxiety. Those were the only moments that felt even slightly safe—a stolen pocket of peace in a life full of storms.

But even that got twisted.

Later, I learned that people had been talking, saying I was "not myself" whenever they were around. In a way, they were right— but not for the reasons they believed.

They didn't know that my silence came from fear.
They didn't know that every time I spoke up to protect my daughter, it was turned against me.
They didn't know that my quietness was my last defense against people who used my words as weapons.

Those fears were too dangerous to share out loud. Anything I said could—and would—be used against me.

Then came another blow.

One day, Miss Louis contacted me. Her tone was sharp and accusing. She said that Miss McClony was unhappy with me because of the way I acted—quiet, withdrawn—as if I was pretending to be abused.

The irony cut deeply.

I was quiet because no one took my fears seriously. Because when I had spoken up about how the other children treated my daughter, my concerns had been dismissed as an overreaction.

My silence was not an act. It was the result of knowing that my child was not safe and that the adults around me did not care.

Trying to reach whatever was left of her conscience, I asked her one simple question:

"Would you be happy if everything you are saying and defending happened to your own daughter?" There was a long, heavy silence.

She didn't answer. She changed the subject. The truth was too uncomfortable to face—because if she admitted it would hurt her own child, she would have to admit it was wrong to let it happen to mine.

Things only got worse.

One afternoon, my daughter tried to walk into Miss McClony's house. One of the older daughters stood at the door and, instead of stopping her gently, she pushed her—hard.

My little girl's head hit the floor with a sickening thud.

For a terrifying moment, she didn't move. She lay there, still and quiet. A cold wave of dread crashed over me. I thought I had lost her.

Then she cried—a sharp, painful, heart-wrenching cry.

I grabbed her, held her close, and we both cried together. The fear of losing her in that moment is something I still carry inside me. After that, I tried to be invisible. I walked carefully. Spoke less. Avoided any conflict. Not because I was weak, but because I knew that any flare-up, any complaint, could make things even worse for both of us.

But hardship didn't need my help to find us.

One day, my daughter complained of a headache. I decided to take her for a walk, hoping the fresh air might ease her pain. I carried her on my back, her small body resting against mine. As we walked, the sky opened and rain poured down. We rushed back to the house, soaked and shivering, hoping for the simple kindness of shelter.

When we reached the door, it was locked.

I knocked. I called. The rain pounded against the roof, mixing with my voice. No one answered. I went to the window and peered inside.

They were there.

Laughing. Moving around. Carrying on as if they couldn't hear me at all. My daughter was cold. I was drenched. And still, no one opened the door.

Only after the rain stopped did they finally unlock it. They told me they "hadn't heard" my knocking. Their excuse sounded as thin as the clothes clinging to my wet skin. By then, my life felt like an unending night. Every attempt to rebuild was torn down. Each time I tried to stand, another blow came. Peace

wasn't just distant—it felt almost imaginary.

In my desperation, I looked anywhere for answers.

I began visiting traditional healers and prophets, using what little money I had to seek some explanation, some spiritual reason, some hope that my life could change. I wanted to believe that someone, somewhere, had the power to break this chain of suffering.

But the more I searched, the more my money disappeared.

I lived in constant anxiety, my eyes often filled with tears as I wondered how we would survive the next day, or the next week. My only fixed income was the R800 I received for my work—barely enough for survival, and yet even that was soon claimed by another crisis.

Then, one day, I received a Facebook message from my cousin. He bluntly asked if I had heard that my brother had gone mad and been arrested. The cold way he delivered the news made it perfectly clear there was no real family connection or empathy left between us. He simply told me to ask my mother about it, which I did.

I was crushed to hear the raw pain in my mother's voice. Nobody was standing with her, and I was far away, struggling just to keep my own head above water.

Without thinking twice, I sent my entire month's salary home.

Every cent of that R800 went to help my family deal with his situation. Once again, my daughter and I were left with nothing. We survived only by the grace of God, clinging to the thin thread of faith that somehow, some way, things would not always be this hard.

On top of that, I had made another mistake.

In a moment of trust—and hope—I had given R500 to Miss Louis. She had promised to return it with interest at monthend. That money was a large part of what little I had, but I was desperate for a way to stretch it. When I later asked for it, needing it back badly, she coldly told me there would be no interest. Only the principal. No apology. No sense of guilt. Just another broken promise.

At the end of the month, she finally returned the R500. It wasn't what she had promised, but still, I felt a small wave of relief. In a life where so much had been taken, simply getting back what belonged to me felt like a rare win.

But Miss Louis's cruelty went far beyond money; she weaponized my respect to destroy me without me ever doing her any wrong. I saw this clearly at a funeral we attended. She walked up to me and hissed that I was dressed like a "bitch." Mortified, I ended up covering my dress so others wouldn't hear her insults.

While still at the funeral, she asked me to fetch some lemons from Miss McClony's garden. When I went looking for the keys and couldn't find them, she told me to just jump over the high wall. She promised she wouldn't tell anyone, since I was only doing it to help her. Out of respect, I did exactly as she asked.

Later, I was utterly stunned to learn that she had gone straight to the elders and told them I had jumped the wall for absolutely no reason. She framed me to look wild and unruly. The embarrassment was so heavy that I had to leave the funeral entirely.

My daughter's fear.
My constant anxiety.
The emotional and financial strain.
The betrayals, one after another.

I was running on empty—but still moving. Still fighting. Still holding my child and believing, however weakly, that this could not be the end of our story.

28

CHAPTER 28

SEEDS OF HOPE, HARVESTS OF BETRAYAL

With my finances hanging by a thread, I knew I couldn't survive on small stipends forever.

The idea of starting a tiny business began to grow quietly in my mind—a small dream of independence in a life where I had depended on too many people who used that dependence against me.

I first approached Miss Mclony, asking if I could run a small business from her yard.

I hoped that, if she allowed it, I could earn just enough to stand on my own feet and maybe even contribute more meaningfully.

She refused without hesitation. No discussion. No alternatives. Just a flat no.

I swallowed the disappointment and tried again.

This time, I went to Miss Louis's sister. To my surprise, she agreed—but with a strange warning.

She said that if anything went wrong, she would not be held responsible.

I didn't fully understand what she meant at the time, but something in her tone made me uneasy. It was as if she already knew the outcome wouldn't be good.

Still, I had to try.

To avoid causing conflict between her and Miss Mclony—who were related—I decided not to sell the goods myself. Instead, I asked the daughter to help sell my small stock.

But it didn't take long for the same old pattern to repeat.

Soon, whispers began to spread. People said that Miss Louis's sister was complaining that I was "eating her food." There was no truth in it, but the rumour was enough to stain my name and make my position even more fragile.

I realised I was being set up for trouble.

Before things could escalate further, I made the painful decision to stop the business completely. It meant losing my small chance at income, but I could see the writing on the wall.

When I asked her daughter for the money from the sales, my request was met with silence.

No explanation. No apology. No payment.

Once again, my effort and trust had turned into unpaid labour for someone else.

Still, hope is stubborn.

After losing that business money, I shifted my focus to something new: gardening.

I asked Miss Louis's sister if I could start a garden in her yard, working alongside her children. Unlike at Miss Mclony's place, there were no chickens to destroy the plants. She agreed, and I allowed myself a tiny spark of excitement.

We started digging garden beds together.

We prepared the soil, planned where to plant what, and for a brief moment, it felt like I was building something of my own. Something that could grow—literally and figuratively.

But then, things took another strange turn.

I noticed that her family kept going to collect manure with Miss Louis, and something about how they did it made me feel like I was being kept at a distance. So, I decided to start my own small garden space separately.

I dug a little well so I could water my plants and began

planting. To my surprise, the garden flourished.

The plants grew strong and green. For the first time in a while, I could look at something and see life, growth, and a future harvest—something no one could easily take away.

Then one day, Miss Louis came to visit.

I hoped she might be happy for me, maybe even proud that I was trying to build something for myself instead of constantly asking for help.

"How does my garden look?" I asked, searching her face for a hint of encouragement.

She looked at my thriving vegetables and shrugged.

"You're wasting your time," she said flatly. "Miss McClony is going to plant maize in the whole garden. You should just remove all of this."

Her words hit me like a stone.

I stood there, looking at the plants I had watered, tended, and hoped in, and felt my heart sink. Once again, something I tried to build was being dismissed and threatened before it even had a chance to fully bloom.

Believing her, I let the garden die.

I stopped caring for it. I stopped watering it. The plants slowly withered, not just from neglect, but from the heavy weight of yet another shattered hope.

Then, some time later, Miss McClony came to visit.

I asked her, cautiously, about her supposed plan to plant maize in the entire garden. She looked at me, surprised, and denied it completely.

At that moment, the truth hit me hard.

Miss Louis had lied.

Not to protect me. Not to help me. But to destroy something that was mine. Something that gave me hope. She had once again chosen to tear down instead of build up.

I tried to salvage what I could from the garden after that, but it never returned to the rich, thriving life it had before.

There are some losses you can't fully reverse, no matter how hard you try.

Then, one day, the past came knocking—literally.

There was a knock at the gate, and when I opened it, I froze.

Standing there was Miss Loveness's husband—the same man who had once helped throw me out of their home like I was nothing. The memory of that humiliation was still sharp.

But this time, he came with a different tone.

He apologised.

He said he was facing serious family problems and needed my help. It was a strange twist of fate, to say the least. I asked why he didn't go to Miss Louis and her sister, he replied that they didn't even know how to begin helping with his situation.

Despite everything he had done to me, something softened inside.

I chose compassion over resentment.

With my baby on my back, I walked with him, guiding him to the places where he could get the help he needed. I didn't do it because he deserved it—I did it because I knew what it meant to need help and find no one.

Later, Louis's sister called to say he had received assistance.

When I gently asked what the outcome had been, she quickly shut down the conversation, saying it was "confidential."

It was strange. I had been the one who helped him access support, yet now I was cut out of even the basic information.

Still, something important had happened that day.

His apology did not erase the past, but it released something heavy inside me. Forgiving him didn't make what he did right— but it made my heart a little lighter.

It reminded me that I wanted to be the kind of person who helped, even when help had not always been returned to me.

Not long after, another incident revealed how one-sided kindness could be in that community.

One day, Miss Louis' niece asked to use Miss Mclony's washing machine.

She had a huge pile of laundry, and I could see she was overwhelmed. Wanting to be kind, I agreed and let her use the machine.

When I returned later, the machine was broken.

She had claimed she knew how to use it. Clearly, she didn't. I told Miss Louis's sister about the damage, and she told me to get it repaired, promising she would repay the cost.

So I did.

I dug into the little I had, paid for the repair, and waited for the money she had promised.

It never came.

I thought about asking, but by then I knew how these things worked. Asking for simple fairness would only paint me as demanding or ungrateful. So I stayed quiet, absorbing yet another small injustice on top of many bigger ones.

Each act on its own might have seemed small—unpaid money, broken trust, a dead garden.

But together, they formed a pattern:

People took what they could from me—time, labour, trust, money, even ideas—and gave back very little, if anything at all.

Yet somehow, through all of it, I kept planting—seeds, efforts, forgiveness. Even when the harvest was betrayal.

Because deep down, I still believed there had to come a season when something I planted would finally grow and not be destroyed.

29

CHAPTER 29

LOVE, VIOLENCE, AND JUSTICE DENIED

For two long years, I lived inside Miss Mclony's yard like a quiet ghost.

I kept to myself, staying mostly in my room. It was my shelter and my prison. After everything I had been through, I had no energy left for friendships, trust, or small talk. Distance felt safer than disappointment.

But even in isolation, the human need for connection doesn't disappear.

Eventually, a small courage rose inside me. I went back to Miss Mclony and asked again if I could start a small business from her home. I needed more than just survival—I needed some independence. Some sense of purpose.

This time, she agreed.

Relief washed over me. I threw myself into work. I stocked what I could, served customers, and slowly, my small business began to grow. For the first time in a very long time, something in my life was actually working.

That's when Mr. Victor appeared.

He started helping me with stocking, giving advice, and just... being there. He was kind. Respectful. Present. In a world where most people had taken from me, he gave—time, energy, attention.

Our conversations became a bright spot in my days.

As weeks turned into months, his visits grew more frequent. His interest shifted from friendly to romantic. At thirty, as a single mother who had endured years of loneliness and rejection, his attention touched a deep ache inside me.

Cautiously, I let my guard down.

I decided to give him a chance, hoping that maybe, just maybe, this connection could lead to something good. I had no idea how quickly that hope would be used against me.

My business was thriving.

Customers came. Stock moved. I was finally starting to feel like I had some control over my life. And with that came a small sense of joy. I laughed more. I talked more. I allowed myself to feel human again.

Then, as before, everything changed after a visit.

One day, Miss McClony returned from seeing Miss Louis. The familiar chill set in. Her eyes were cold, her posture stiff, her tone charged with anger.

She confronted me about Mr. Victor.

Her words were sharp, full of judgment and insult. It wasn't concern—it was condemnation. She attacked my character, my choices, my right to even consider love.

Tired of always defending myself to people determined to misunderstand me, I chose silence.

I retreated to my room, hoping the storm would pass if I stayed out of the way.

But the next day, the storm arrived at my door.

The woman who had carried tales about my relationship with Mr. Victor showed up at the yard, wearing her smugness like perfume.

She started talking loudly, revealing personal details about my life—details meant to shame and hurt.

I tried to defend myself, calmly reminding her that my personal life was my own. But she didn't stop. Instead, she dug further.

She criticised Mr. Victor's age and background.
She mocked me—my quietness, my walk, my way of speaking. To her, I wasn't a person. I was an easy target.

I felt deeply underestimated and insulted.

Her verbal attack escalated until she threatened to beat me. Something in me rose up. I was done being a doormat. I stood my ground, prepared to defend myself if I had to.

But I didn't expect what happened next.

Before we could even face each other, Miss McClony stepped in—not as a peacemaker, but as an attacker.

Fueled by gossip, misunderstanding, and her own bitterness, she began to slap me. Hard. Repeatedly.

The hits came fast.

Stunned and hurting, I chose not to hit back. I stepped outside, hoping that moving away would calm things down.

It didn't.

She followed me, now holding a large stick in her hand.

Fear rushed through my body—not for myself, but for my daughter.

I knew that if I tried to run or fight back, her anger could easily turn on my child. I couldn't risk that. I couldn't let my daughter be the target of her rage.

So I made a decision only a mother truly understands:

I used my own body as a shield.

As she began beating me with the stick, I twisted and turned to keep my daughter behind me, out of her reach. Every blow landed on me instead of her.

The pain was unbearable.

My cries of agony mixed with my daughter's terrified screams. The sound echoed across the compound, finally catching the attention of people nearby who were playing dice.

They saw enough to know this was not a simple argument.

They called the police.

By the time the officers arrived, the beating had stopped.

I was still standing, but every part of me ached. My body felt heavy, bruised, and weak. As I walked slowly toward the police van, the world around me began to blur.

The sounds grew distant.

The colours faded.
Then everything went black.

When I woke up, cold water was being splashed onto my face.

I lay under the shade of a tree. My clothes were soaked. My vision was hazy, and faces hovered around me in a blur of concern and curiosity. I felt completely exposed—physically, emotionally, spiritually.

Not long after, I was called over to where the officers stood with Miss Mclony and Miss Louis.

Mr. Victor tried to come too. He had seen what happened. He wanted to speak up for me. But the officers stopped him.

They said only “family” could be present.

I had no family there.

The message was clear: in this circle, I stood alone.

They asked me what happened.

I told them. I explained how the argument started, how I was beaten, how I had done nothing to justify that kind of violence. My voice shook, but I spoke my truth.

Their response was weak and empty.

They simply told us to “treat each other with kindness” in the future, as if I had just been part of a simple disagreement—not the victim of a brutal assault.

Then came the final betrayal of that moment.

Miss Louis spoke up.

She told the officers that I was disrespectful, that I had deserved what happened. She even claimed she had seen the whole thing and that it was “just a slap.” A lie.

I remembered clearly: she only arrived after I had already collapsed and been revived. She had not seen the attack. She had not heard my screams. She had not watched me shield my daughter with my own body.

But her words carried more weight than my wounds.

The officers barely looked at my injuries. They didn’t push further. They didn’t challenge her lies.

There would be no real justice that day.

After they left, the atmosphere grew even darker.

Instead of calming down, Miss McClony and Miss Louis became bolder. They sat me down and unleashed a cruel barrage of words.

They told me I would never become anything.
That I would fall into drugs.
That I would drag my daughter down with me.
That my future was hopeless.

Their words tried to finish what the stick had started.

But even as my body throbbed with pain and my spirit felt crushed, something deep inside me refused to accept their prophecy over my life.

They saw a broken, beaten woman with no one to stand for her.

They did not see what God saw.
They did not see what time would reveal.
They did not see that I was still standing—again.

Bleeding. Hurt. Humiliated.
But still standing.

30

CHAPTER 30

REVENGE WITHOUT REMORSE: BEATEN, BLAMED, AND CAST OUT

Their laughter hurt almost as much as the blows.

After the police left and the dust of the chaos settled, everyone present took turns mocking me. I sat there weeping quietly, trying to piece together what sin I had committed that could possibly justify such cruelty.

They attacked me for daring to seek companionship with Mr.
Victor.

They labelled him a thief without a single piece of evidence.

Their judgments were loud and absolute, yet their own lives were full of contradictions. Many of them, rumoured to be foreigners with fraudulent South African documents, had access to grants and opportunities that genuine citizens often struggled to receive.

Their children were far from innocent.

Some had relationships with multiple men, including married ones. Rumours whispered of abortions and secret scandals. But none of that was discussed openly. None of them were dragged into the light and humiliated the way I was.

For me, however, they reserved public shame.

If I had truly erred, a private conversation, a gentle correction, or even a firm warning would have been human. Instead, they chose a beating in front of my child and a crowd.

They chose to strip me of my dignity.

Miss Mclony's words cut deeper than the stick she had used.

She reminded me, in front of everyone, how I had arrived at her home—calling me a "street kid," mocking my "smelly clothes" and "unkempt hair." Her words turned my desperation into a joke, something people could laugh at.

And they did.

Some of the onlookers chuckled as she painted that degrading picture. Their laughter wrapped around me like chains. It felt as though I was cursed, destined for humiliation no matter how hard I tried to rise.

Her cruelty pulled up old memories—times I had felt worthless, abandoned, and unwanted. Each word reopened old wounds I thought I had learned to live with.

Deep down, I knew what was coming next.

I had seen this pattern too many times:
First the conflict.
Then the shaming.
Then the silent decision to cast me out.

I began mentally preparing myself for another eviction—even as my body still screamed from the pain of the beating. My back throbbed. My energy was drained. Even trying to sell my small stock felt impossible.

Hopelessness hovered over me like a dark cloud.

Then came the "forgiveness."

They put on an act of calm, spoke softly, and pretended everything was under control. They used careful words, as if to say, “Let’s move on.” But my spirit was not fooled.

Beneath their calm, danger simmered.

I could feel it most strongly around certain relatives of Miss
Mclony. Their eyes followed me with suspicion and judgment, their whispering never far behind. My instincts screamed that I was not safe.

And, once again, my instincts were right.

I learned that Miss Louis had continued her quiet campaign against me.

She had been twisting my words, taking bits of conversations and reshaping them to feed conflict. She didn’t just gossip—she engineered drama. She stirred suspicion like it was her calling.

Her motives were never clear, but one thing was:
She enjoyed the harm she caused.

Barely a week after the beating, another horrifying truth came to light.

I discovered that Miss Louis's sister —the same woman who still owed me money—had been openly bragging. She had apparently told others that she had encouraged Miss McClony to beat me.

Worse still, she had said that if I dared to fight back, she was ready to join forces with Miss Louis to "teach me a lesson." The chill that ran through me was deep.

It hit me that my choice not to fight physically, my decision to respect my elders even when they didn't deserve it, had likely saved me from an even more dangerous attack.

They saw my restraint as weakness.
But in reality, it was my shield.

Toward the end of the month, something unexpected happened.

One evening, Miss McClony returned with her husband. I greeted her politely, trying to carry on with some trace of normalcy despite everything that had happened.

That night, she cried.

Not a few quiet tears, but the whole night through. Her sobbing echoed in the house. I lay there listening, stunned and confused.

I was the one whose body had been battered.
I was the one who had been bleeding since the assault.
I was the one whose back throbbed with constant pain.

Yet she was the one weeping.

Her tears felt like a strange kind of performance—an expression of guilt she would never admit, or a battle inside herself that I had no access to. Either way, they did nothing to ease my reality.

The next morning, the blow I had been expecting finally came.

Her husband, blunt and emotionless, told me that my services were no longer needed. His sister was coming to stay in the house.

Just like that, I was out.

Homeless. Again.

A heavy wave of despair washed over me. Where would I go this time? How many more times would I have to start again? The idea of staying with another man, after everything I'd been through, filled me with dread.

I felt like a pawn in a game I hadn't agreed to play.

Later that day, they returned with the sister-in-law.

When I saw them approaching, I knew my time there was officially over. As they came closer, Miss McClony gave me a small, tight smile.

It did not feel kind.

It felt like victory—hers, not mine.

Tears burned my eyes. She had hurt me, humiliated me, and now officially replaced me. In her mind, justice had been served.

In mine, justice had been completely denied.

Soon, I learned that my eviction was no secret.

Some of her friends confidently announced that they had known I would be "fired." They said it with no shame, no empathy. Just satisfaction, like spectators at a show.

These were adults. Mothers. Women with daughters of their own who could easily make mistakes and need compassion one day.

Yet they celebrated my downfall.

What stung most was realising I had become their enemy simply because I dared to want more for myself. Because I was trying to build a better life. Because I had a small business. Because my customers saw me, cared for me, and supported me.

My progress offended them.

Since the day of the beating, my body had not been the same.

My back pain refused to leave. I relied on traditional herbs and whatever painkillers I could manage to buy, just to make it through each day. It was not enough.

Sometimes, late at night, a deep fear whispered inside me:

What if this pain grows into something worse?
What if one day, the damage they caused becomes lifethreatening?
What if their violence doesn't just mark my past—but my future too?

Every ache in my back became a reminder.

Not only of what they had done to me, but of how easily they walked away from it. Unpunished. Unquestioned. Unchanged.

They got their revenge.

I was left with the pain.

Yet even in that pain, one truth remained:

They had not destroyed me.

Bruised, betrayed, exhausted, and once again displaced—I was still alive. Still thinking. Still hoping, however faintly, for a life beyond their cruelty.

31

CHAPTER 31

A WEB OF DECEIT: HOMELESS, HURTING, AND SABOTAGED

Homelessness visited me again like an old, unwelcome friend.

Once more, I had nowhere to sleep—not even for a single night. Under pressure from Miss Mclony, I moved my few belongings to a nearby hair salon, using it as a temporary storage space
while my mind raced for solutions.

Every option I considered closed in front of me.

In that moment of crisis, Mr. Victor—who had once been a steady presence—was nowhere to be seen. His absence stung, adding another layer of abandonment to my already fragile state.

But in the middle of that darkness, a faint light appeared.

Although he didn't show up at first, Mr. Victor had spoken to his friend, Mr. Abel. Through him, a door cracked open: Mr. Abel offered me one of his rooms to use.

It was a potential long-term answer—but it didn't solve the immediate problem of where I would sleep that night.

As a heavy rainstorm rolled in, I took shelter at the same salon where my belongings were stored. The sound of the rain beating on the roof matched the heaviness in my chest.

A woman who lived nearby noticed me.

She saw my soaked clothes, my exhausted posture, the weight of everything I'd been carrying. Moved by compassion, she invited me into her home for the night.

By then, the physical effects of the beating from Miss McClony were getting worse.

The pain was intense. I was bleeding heavily, and it frightened me. The woman who helped me could see something was seriously wrong and gently asked what had happened. Her concern was a rare kindness in a season full of cruelty.

The next day, a tiny seed of hope was planted.

Mr. Victor finally appeared. He gathered some of his friends, and together they built a small shack in the yard of the woman who had given me shelter. It would serve as a space for my business—a new beginning.

I used the last of my savings to restock.

Every coin I had left went into that small venture. I poured what remained of my strength and hope into it, praying that this time, my efforts would bear fruit.

But starting from scratch is never simple.

The room Mr. Abel had offered me was far from where my business stood. The yard itself needed serious cleaning before I could move in properly. My body, still weak and bleeding, wouldn't let me do much physical work.

I was afraid to speak up about my health.

I didn't know how people would react if I admitted how bad things really were. Fear of judgment kept me quiet, even as my body cried out for rest and care.

For a short while, I stayed in the woman's house.

More than anything, I wanted to stand on my own feet—and still be close to people, even if they had no idea what I was going through.

Eventually, I moved into the room and kept doing business from the woman's yard.

But as time went on, something didn't add up.

My business never seemed to grow. My stock decreased, but the money wasn't matching the losses. It felt as if my goods
were disappearing into thin air.

No matter how hard I tried, my small venture refused to move forward. Slowly, painfully, it ground to a complete halt. Once again, my attempt at building stability slipped through my fingers.

Then came another familiar pattern: a visit and a sudden change.

One day, Miss Louis came to see the husband of the woman who had helped me. Their conversation was quiet, their tones low, but the atmosphere around them felt heavy.

I couldn't hear what they were saying, but I didn't need to.

My spirit sensed it: trouble.

Not long after she left, the husband called me over. His attitude had changed. He told me he no longer wanted my business operating on his property.

Just like that, the welcome was withdrawn.

I tried to understand. I asked why. He spoke vaguely about

not wanting to be held responsible if I fell sick or died on his property. His words were extreme, out of proportion to the quiet way I had been running my business.

In my heart, I knew what had happened.

This was not about illness or death. This was about influence.

I could feel Miss Louis's fingerprints all over this decision. Her presence had again turned kindness into suspicion.

With no other choice, I dismantled my little shack.

The structure that had carried so much of my renewed hope was taken apart, reduced to sheets of corrugated iron and pieces of wood. It felt like watching my dreams being disassembled.

Mr. Victor helped me once more.

He assisted in moving the shack materials to a yard near, a more distant home. It was far from where I usually moved, but at that point, distance meant little compared to simply having somewhere to try again.

Because of the distance, he arranged for a man who lived closer to store my remaining stock.

It was a practical solution—but it also meant I had to trust yet another person with the little I had left. After so many betrayals, that wasn't easy.

Standing in that new, distant place, I felt tired—but not entirely defeated.

Yet again, I had been pushed out.
Yet again, my hard work had been sabotaged.
Yet again, people had allowed one woman's poison to shape their choices.

But somehow, despite all of that, a small part of me still refused to give up completely.

Because as long as I had breath, I still had a chance—even if the world around me kept trying to silence it.

32

CHAPTER 32

A CHANCE ENCOUNTER, A BROKEN BOUNDARY, AND A HIDDEN ENEMY

Piece by piece, I tried to rebuild.

After scraping together money from small piece jobs, I finally managed to restock and restart my business in a new location. It wasn't much, but it was hope. On that very first day of trading, though, something happened that sent a cold shiver down my spine.

I walked past the road where Miss Louis lived.

I had been avoiding her on purpose, trying to protect my peace by keeping my distance from her and the chaos she carried with her. But as I passed, she called out my name.

I didn't want to respond.

Every part of me wanted to keep walking, but I turned back. Years of conditioning to "respect elders" tugged against my instinct to protect myself.

She told me my mother had sent her a WhatsApp message.

Then she casually admitted that she had taken it upon herself to tell my mother about my struggles—about how much I was suffering.

My heart sank.

I had deliberately hidden the extent of my hardships from my mother. Not because I didn't trust her, but because I loved her. She was far away, with no way to practically help, and I didn't want her drowning in worry and helplessness.

For Miss Louis to break that boundary without my consent felt like a deep violation.

I had physically moved away from her, tried to distance myself from her influence, yet she still found ways to insert herself into my life and decisions.

When I asked what exactly she had told my mother, her answers were vague and evasive.

Knowing her talent for lies and exaggeration, I had no confidence that my mother had received a fair or accurate picture.

That thought haunted me: my mother sitting far away, imagining the worst, based on words that might not even be true.

I walked away from that encounter unsettled, but I forced myself to refocus.

I had to keep going. I had a business to run. A child to feed. A life to fight for.

At first, things went surprisingly well.

Customers came. Sales trickled in. I slowly began to see some return on my small investment. I even managed to get a sturdy wooden container to store and protect my stock—a small but meaningful step toward security.

Then, without warning, it all shattered.

Someone broke into the container. The lock was forced open. My goods were stolen.

The little I had built up was torn away again.

I went to Mr. Pat, the owner of the property where my stock was kept. I asked him what had happened, hoping for some explanation, maybe even support.

He had none.

His answers were unsatisfactory, disconnected, as if my loss was a small inconvenience not worth his time. I walked away feeling robbed twice—first by the thief, then by his indifference.

Still, my business was all I had.

Even in its fragile state, it was my only real means of survival. I clung to it, even as people around me began forming wrong ideas.

Some started assuming that because I had a shack and stock, I must be making a lot of money.

They didn't see the reality: constant risk, small profit, frequent loss. Their misconceptions would soon become another
weapon turned against me.

One day, while I was serving customers, I heard shouting.

A neighbour stormed over, his face twisted with anger. He shouted that I was running a business on "his property" without his permission.

At first, I tried to ignore it.

I hoped that silence would cool things down. But it didn't. His anger escalated. His words grew darker, sharper, more dangerous.

Then he said it.

He threatened to kill me and my daughter if I didn't remove my shack immediately.

Those words cut through me like a blade.

Memories of past violence, of beatings and near-death fear, rushed back. I knew from experience that threats like that couldn't be taken lightly.

Shaking, I reached for the only help I could think of: Mr. Victor.

He responded quickly and came to where I was. He tried to speak to the man, to calm him down, to meditate in some way. But the neighbour's rage didn't stop.

He hurled insults—not just at me, but at my parents, people he had never met. His voice grew louder and more hateful, while I stood there holding onto my self-control like a lifeline.

I refused to engage with his insults.

I stayed silent, not because I was weak, but because I was tired of having my reactions used against me. I had put too much effort into rebuilding to let another person's baseless hatred push me out without a fight.

Later, pieces of the truth found their way to me.

Several people, who had seen more than I realised, came to me quietly. They told me they had seen that same neighbour meeting with Miss Louis multiple times before his outburst.

Suddenly, everything made sense.

This wasn't random anger. It was directed. Fuelled. Encouraged.

Once again, the same shadowy hand was behind the chaos.

My enemy wasn't just the man who shouted at me. It was the woman who kept working from the background, pulling strings, planting poison, and turning others against me.

People in the community began asking me a question I couldn't answer.

"What did you do to her?"

Their voices were full of confusion and concern. They couldn't understand why she seemed so determined to make my life miserable.

The truth was simple and painful: I didn't know either.

I had never intentionally wronged her. I had shown her respect. Trusted her. Even given her money. Yet she moved through my life like a storm, targeting whatever scraps of stability I managed to build.

I didn't have the luxury of investigating her motives.

I had no money for lawyers. No time for drama. No emotional strength left for trying to decode someone else's darkness.

All I could do was focus on what I did have control over:

Keeping my business going,
Staying alive,
And protecting my child.

Her hatred became another background noise in a life already filled with sirens.

I couldn't silence it.
I couldn't understand it.
But I refused to let it completely define me.

I chose to keep moving forward—one step, one sale, one day at a time.

33

CHAPTER 33

WHEN "HELP" HAS A PRICE: DEBT, DESIRE, AND STOLEN DREAMS

In yet another attempt to rebuild, I went back to the basics.

I needed stock. Without enough goods to sell, there was no business, no income, no way to feed my child. So I did the only thing that made sense—I went to Mr. Pat and asked for the money he owed me.

I thought it was a simple, fair request.

Instead, it triggered another disaster.

His reaction was instant and harsh. He refused to pay, insisting that the money was actually owed to him as "rent."

Then, without warning, he told me to pack my things and leave his place immediately.

He even brought up an old story to make me feel guilty.

He claimed that when he needed help financially, I had refused him. But the truth was different. I had gone door-to-door in the community for him, humbly asking people if they could lend him money. No one had helped—but it was not for lack of trying on my part.

Still, he chose to rewrite the story in a way that painted me as selfish and ungrateful.

What pierced me most wasn't just his refusal—it was his expectations.

Despite seeing my constant struggle, despite knowing I was barely surviving, he somehow believed I was in a position to provide him with financial support.

His own friends and family had failed him. Yet his anger landed on me.

Then he added another layer of insult.

He complained that I didn't clean his house or wash his dishes, as if that had ever been part of our agreement. It was as though, in his mind, allowing me to keep stock on his property meant I automatically owed him my labour and domestic service.

The truth was simple: we had never agreed to that.

Yes, when I arrived each morning to set up for business, I would quickly tidy the place—straighten things, place the dishes neatly, just as a gesture of respect. But I didn't have the time, strength, or obligation to be his maid.

He even complained that I didn't make his bed.

I was not his wife. I was not his employee. I was a struggling mother trying to run a business from his space. His expectations
were not only unreasonable, they were deeply disrespectful.

Then came the most disturbing part.

In a strange, unsettling moment, he confessed that he had been "showing me love" in his own way—but I hadn't noticed.

His words turned my stomach.

It suddenly became clear: underneath his anger, there was something else. Something inappropriate. My vulnerability— my lack of power, my need for space—had made me easy to target.

I wasn't just cheap labour.
I was someone he thought he could claim.

Once again, my struggle for survival had been mistaken for availability—for access, for ownership, for control.

With the help of a friend, I gathered what was left of my belongings.

We moved my things outside his house and placed them near the gate. It was already humiliating. Then he came out, looked at my possessions, and called them "rubbish."

He ordered me to move my "rubbish" away from his property. His words were like a slap to the soul.

With no other options, we loaded my things into a rickety wheelbarrow and started down the road. The sky was getting darker, and the path was bumpy and uneven.

At one point, I stumbled.

The weight of the wheelbarrow nearly took me down with it. I almost broke my leg trying to keep everything from spilling into the dirt.

That moment summed up my entire life:

Carrying heavy burdens in the dark, on an unstable path, with no one truly helping to balance the load.

Back in my small room, the reality hit hard.

Food was almost gone. What remained was my leftover stock— the same goods meant to build a business were now my only hope of survival.

I decided to dismantle the business shack one last time.

Taking it apart felt like taking apart my own dreams, piece by piece. I shifted my focus to finding piece jobs—anything I could do for a bit of cash.

My dream of running a small, independent business had become too painful to keep chasing.

Then came the final insult—the kind that doesn't break your bones but strikes your spirit.

Soon after I took down my shack, I heard something in the community that made my blood run cold: Miss Louis had started the exact same business I had been running.

Same idea.

Same setup.

Same kind of stock.

It was not a coincidence.

At that moment, everything snapped into focus.

All the sabotage, the quiet attacks, the poisoned conversations, the efforts to get me chased from one place to another—it wasn't random. It wasn't just personal hatred.

It was business.

She had watched me build something from nothing, then decided she wanted it for herself—without the suffering, without the risks, without the instability.

She took my idea and tried to erase me from it.

She didn't care that I had no support.
No safety net.
No husband.
No stable income.

She didn't care that I was clinging to that business as my only way to feed my child.

She had a house, a husband, and stability—and still, she wanted my little source of survival.

That month was brutal.

I struggled to eat. Every day was a negotiation between hunger, exhaustion, and forced resilience. It shocked me how relentless she was in squeezing out every last rand of profit she could— from a space she knew I had once depended on just to stay alive.

Her behaviour finally exposed her motive clearly:

It was not just gossip.
Not just drama.
Not even just jealousy.

It was envy mixed with a desire to destroy anything that gave me a chance to rise.

Eventually, fear began to grow inside me—not just of what she had already done, but of what she might still be capable of.

The thought of trying to rebuild yet another business filled me with dread.

What if she sabotaged it again?
What if her next move was worse?
What if staying visible as a businesswoman was actually putting my life and my child at risk?

So I let the dream go.

I released it with trembling hands, not because I didn't want it, but because survival demanded another path. I turned fully to piece jobs—unpredictable, unstable, but less visible, less threatening to those who wanted to compete by destroying.

In that quieter, less noticeable life, something unexpected appeared:

A fragile, small sense of peace.

People no longer watched me as closely. The direct harassment slowed. I worked when and where I could, earning just enough to cover the basics.

It was not the life I had dreamed of.

But through those odd jobs, I managed to feed my child. I managed to keep a roof over our heads. I managed, in a quiet, hidden way, to keep going.

Not thriving.
Not shining.
But surviving.

And sometimes, in the aftermath of repeated storms, survival itself is a quiet kind of victory.

34

CHAPTER 34

THE WEIGHT OF SCORN AND THE PRICE OF DESPERATION

I sat in my small room, holding onto hope the way some people hold their breath underwater.

I was broke. No savings. No backup. No one to call. My only option was to search for piece jobs wherever I could find them. Each small task I landed kept us one step away from total collapse.

Then I heard a rumour.

Someone in the area was lending money. For most people, it was just talk. For me, it sounded like a lifeline.

I went to her house, my heart pounding with a mix of fear and hope.

When I arrived, she wasn't there. Instead, I found my neighbour, Zandile, working as her assistant. She told me to come back another time. I left quietly, already rehearsing how I would explain my situation when I returned.

The next morning, I saw something that made my heart sink.

I watched as Zandile laughed and warmly shook hands with another neighbour, Thuli. At first, I told myself it was none of my business. People were allowed to talk, to laugh, to live freely.

Then Thuli walked straight toward me.

"Why would you embarrass yourself, borrowing money?" she sneered. "She won't give you anything. You're not working, and you're not even a citizen." At that moment, everything clicked.

The laughter. The handshake. The looks.

They had been talking about me.

My face burned. I felt so small, like the ground was opening beneath me. I had nothing to say. The courage it had taken just to try and borrow money was crushed in an instant.

The idea of asking for that loan died right there.

But it didn't stop with that one moment.

Thuli kept spreading her poison around the community. She gossiped about my struggles, mocked my constant cleaning jobs, and said I would get "a lump on my back" from working in other people's homes.

Her words were meant to shame me.

I felt every one of them like a sting—but I kept going. I knew what I wanted: survival, dignity, and a better life for my daughter. If hard work bent my back, at least it was honest
work.

Then she started on my child.

She began mocking my daughter, calling her a slow learner. That cut deeper than anything she had said about me.

For a moment, the world tilted.

I felt despair wash over me. My child had done nothing. She was innocent—just trying to grow in a world that seemed determined to break her mother.

But I had faced worse storms.

I refused to crumble. I held my daughter closer, prayed harder, and reminded myself that God saw everything they didn't—my intentions, my efforts, my heart.

The piece jobs became my lifeline.

But it soon became clear that one odd job here and there would never be enough. I needed several in a single day just to make it to tomorrow.

So, I swallowed my pride again.

I decided to go door-to-door, asking for any work—no matter how small, no matter how humbling. My dignity had already been bruised so many times that asking for help was just another scar.

One day, I walked into a yard where a man was working alone.

He was busy, focused. I approached carefully and asked if he had any piece jobs I could do.

He told me he didn't have any work at that moment.

Then he looked at me, at my tired face, at my child, and seemed to soften. Noticing how worn out and hungry we looked, he offered us food.

We sat and ate rice and beans.

It was simple, but to us, it was a blessing. For a brief moment, I tasted something that felt like kindness—a reminder that not everyone in the world was cruel.

But the conversation began to change.

As we talked, a knot formed in my stomach. His tone shifted. His eyes lingered too long. He started talking about his intimate life—about how long it had been since he had been with a woman.

The air around us felt different. He wasn't just talking. He was preparing me.

Then he said it.

He told me he could give me R30—the small amount he said was somewhere in the house—if I agreed to sleep with him.

It wasn't a hesitant request. It was casual. Assumed. As if my desperation made my body part of the bargain.

I felt shock rise inside me, followed quickly by fear.

I realised I was alone in a yard with a man who saw my hunger as an opportunity. He believed my poverty made me easy to buy.

I didn't argue. I didn't shout.

Instinct kicked in. I pretended to agree, pretending to go along with his plan so he wouldn't become suspicious or aggressive.

He then turned his attention to my baby.

He commented that she was still awake, watching everything. I quickly responded that I would tie her on my back and that she
would soon fall asleep.

My heart was racing.

As soon as I got her securely onto my back, I did the only thing I could:

I ran.

I didn't walk. I didn't hesitate. I bolted out of that yard with all the strength I had left, my legs moving faster than my thoughts, my heart beating so hard I thought it might burst.

I didn't stop to look behind me.

I just ran until I felt some distance between us and him, between us and danger.

When I finally slowed down, my whole body was shaking.

I couldn't breathe properly. My hands trembled. My mind replayed everything he had said like a nightmare I couldn't wake from.

Any courage I had to keep asking for work that day disappeared.

I couldn't go to another house. Couldn't knock on another gate. The encounter had scraped open a fresh wound, reminding me that in my desperation, some people didn't see a woman or a mother.

They saw an opportunity.

I needed time to breathe.
Time to think.
Time to process what I had just escaped.

At that moment, it felt like the world was full of traps.

People mocked me for trying to survive.
They judged me for being poor.
They sexualised my desperation.
They attacked my child with their words.

But even then, one truth remained:

I was still here.

Still refusing to sell my dignity for survival.

Still holding on to God, even when the world showed me its ugliest side.

35

CHAPTER 35

THE MASKS THEY WEAR: HYPOCRISY AND ABUSE

While I was living in my single room, my daughter, Happy, fell ill.

I was exhausted, broke, and scared. I didn't know what to do. My resources were already stretched to breaking point, and now I had a sick child looking up at me with tired eyes.

A kind friend stepped in.

She offered to help me find Happy's father, Peter. Together we went searching for his place, following directions and fragments of memory until we finally found his home.

We were met at the door by a woman I had never seen before— one of his wives.

I explained that Happy was sick, that I needed help, that this wasn't a casual visit. She listened with what looked like sympathy and then calmly told us Peter wasn't there and wouldn't be coming back anytime soon.

But just as she said those words... Peter appeared.

He came out from behind her, destroying her lie in an instant. She let out a strained laugh, as if it were nothing. To her, it might have been a small, awkward moment. To me, it was a slap.

We were there for a serious reason.
Not for games.
Not for deceit.

We went inside and sat down.

As we spoke, I realised something unsettling: Peter's wife knew a lot about me. About my life. About my struggles. Far more than I knew about her. It was as if I had been discussed, examined, and judged long before I ever arrived there.

I stayed quiet.

I chose my words carefully, not wanting to expose more than necessary in front of my friend, and always thinking of Happy's privacy and dignity. My child's safety and reputation meant more to me than my own.

Seeing the reality with her own eyes, my friend was moved.

She watched me—a struggling mother with a sick child and an absent father—and suggested Peter buying food and clothes for Happy. I tried to refuse. My pride was fragile, but it was still there, trying to protect what little sense of self I had left.

But she insisted.

She said she couldn't stand to see us suffering while Peter was alive and clearly able to help. Her words forced the truth into the room: he wasn't dead, missing, or helpless. He was simply choosing not to take responsibility.

Eventually, Peter and his wife agreed to provide food—but there was a limit.

They offered only 1kg of food for Happy.

I felt frustration rise within me. I had spent far more than that on food for us in the past, even when it meant going without for myself. But I held my tongue. I swallowed the anger and chose silence to avoid adding more drama to an already tense situation.

At month-end, Peter suggested something else.

He proposed that we go together to buy clothes for the children—his and Happy. I agreed, hoping this might finally be a step toward him accepting his role as a father.

At the shop, the truth showed itself again.

I was limited to R500 for Happy's clothes. I stretched every rand carefully, choosing only what she truly needed.

His wife, on the other hand, picked clothes for her children freely, with no mention of a budget.

Then, as we stood in the queue, she casually asked him what they would do if the money wasn't enough.

His reply froze me.

He said that if the money ran short, they would simply return my daughter's clothes.

Just like that.

It was as if Happy was an afterthought. As if she were less real, less deserving, less his, than his other children.

A lump formed in my throat.

I wanted to cry, to scream, to ask him how he could talk about his own child like that. But I forced myself to stay outwardly calm, holding my pain inside where they couldn't see it.

What hurt the most was what she didn't know—or didn't care to know.

Peter's wife seemed completely unaware of the sacrifices I had

made for her husband in the past. There were times when I went without food to help support their business. I had poured my energy, my time, my strength into something that benefitted them.

Now, standing there in that line, I was treated as if I were a beggar.

When it came time to pay, his wife went first.

She paid for her children's clothes. I watched carefully, my heart pounding slightly, afraid there might not be enough left for Happy.

But by some grace, there was.

The remaining money was enough to cover the modest clothes I had chosen for my daughter. I felt a fragile wave of relief wash over me.

We returned to their home so I could collect Happy's clothes.

While we were there, a customer arrived—someone who knew Peter but not me. Looking at Happy, he asked Peter who she was.

Peter replied, "It's her daughter, Happy."

Just that. No acknowledgment. No ownership. No mention that she was his child too.

Then the customer turned to me.

His face twisted with disgust, and without knowing anything about my life, he called me a "mad woman" and said I deserved death.

The words struck me like physical blows.

I stood up, my voice shaking slightly, and asked him what I had ever done to deserve such hatred from a stranger.

He didn't answer.

He just turned around and walked away, leaving his cruelty hanging in the air like smoke.

I left their home that day with my heart heavy.

I felt embarrassed. Hurt. Exposed. Once again, I was made to carry the shame that did not belong to me.

But beneath all that pain, there was something unshakable:

I knew my truth.

I knew the kind of mother I was.
I knew the sacrifices I had made.
I knew the love I carried for my child.

And no stranger's insult, no selective father, and no coldhearted wife could take that away from me.

36

CHAPTER 36

THE MASK OF CARE: WHEN "HELP" HIDES CONTROL

Survival forced me into work I never imagined doing.

To bring in anything extra for Happy, I started collecting scrap metal—tins, cans, anything I could find on the streets. The weight of the bags on my shoulders felt like a physical reflection of my life: heavy, dirty, but necessary.

One day, while we were out collecting, a boy approached us.

He was older than Happy, but still a child himself. He started playing with her right in front of me—laughing, talking, acting like any other child might.

After a while, he asked Happy if they could go play at the back of the house, out of my sight.

My instincts flared.

I had lived through too much to ignore that inner warning. I followed quietly, staying just far enough behind so I wouldn't be noticed.

Then I saw it.

He was trying to take off Happy's clothes.

A surge of rage and terror shot through me. My heart pounded in my chest as I rushed forward, shouting, demanding to know what he thought he was doing.

He stammered something I couldn't even fully understand— half excuse, half fear.

But I was clear.

I chased him away and warned him never to come near my child or my place again. The memory of what almost happened burned into me like fire.

Then, life twisted in that strange way it often did.

Not long after, I was introduced to his parents.

A woman I had been washing clothes for connected me with a new opportunity: cleaning work at the home of Miss Thandeka and her husband, Mr. Sithole.

They were the parents of that same boy.

They offered me R500 a month to clean their yard and help with work. To someone standing on the edge of survival, it sounded like a lifeline.

Then came the invitation that made my heart sink.

After some time, Miss Thandeka asked me to move in with them.

Immediately, alarm bells rang inside me. Memories of other homes, other "opportunities," and other kinds of abuse rose to the surface. I knew too well how quickly "help" could turn into control.

I didn't hide my fears.

I told her about what had happened at Miss Mclony's. I told her about the beatings, the humiliation, and the back pain that still haunted me from that time.

She listened and covered her promises in kindness.

She told me I had nothing to worry about. That she was not like those people. That she would treat me well.

But by then, I had learned not to trust words easily.

Still, when the small room I was renting was suddenly put up for sale, I was cornered. I had nowhere else to go with my child.

So, with a heavy heart and a fearful mind, I agreed to move

in. At first, it felt like I had made the right choice.

They gave us a shack to stay in. It wasn't much, but it was at least a roof over our heads and felt safer than some of the places
we had lived before. I was genuinely grateful.

But safety that depends on someone else's mood never lasts long.

The first red flag appeared when my payment was late.

A knot of worry grew in my stomach. I reached out to the woman who had introduced us, hoping she could help bridge the gap and ask what was going on.

When Miss Thandeka eventually came, she was different.

The warmth was gone. Her tone was cold, distant. She gave some vague excuse about being "busy," but my spirit told me something was off.

When she finally handed me the money, it was R100 short.

I had been expecting R500. She gave me R400.

I took a breath and asked, as respectfully as I could, why it was less than what we had agreed on.

She looked me in the eye and lied.

She insisted that R400 had been part of the original agreement. I knew it wasn't true. She knew it wasn't true. The lie sat heavy between us like a stone.

My chest tightened with dread.

I recognised the pattern. It always started like this: a small change, a quiet cheating, a testing of how much they could get away with.

I wanted to stand my ground.

I wanted to demand what was fair. But I also knew the cost of speaking up too strongly when you have nowhere else to go.

Homelessness hovered over me like a threat.

So I swallowed my anger and took the reduced amount.

The following month, things became more obvious.

This time, it was Mr. Sithole who raised the topic of payment. His tone was casual, but his words were not.

He said that people who didn't have a place to stay shouldn't expect to be paid.

The message was crystal clear:
Your "rent" is your silence.
Your "gratitude" is your labour.
Your "home" is our leverage.

I bit my tongue so hard it felt like it might bleed. Any argument, any protest, could easily cost me both my shelter and my work.

That night, lying in the shack they had given us, I stared at the thin walls and felt the old, suffocating feeling again.

Trapped.

It hit me that I had not escaped abuse. I had only changed its address.

The names were different. The promises were different. But the power dynamic was painfully familiar: they had the home, the money, the control. I had the need.

What made it worse was the way Miss Thandeka spoke in public.

She often declared passionately how much she hated people who abused children. She would say, with dramatic conviction, that she would do anything to protect her own—even resort to violence if anyone ever hurt them.

To others, she sounded like a fierce, protective mother.

To me, her words rang hollow.

Because every time she spoke like that, my mind flashed back to the day I found her son trying to undress my daughter.

I had protected Happy that day, chased him away, and drawn a firm line.

She never forgot that.

Beneath her “kindness,” I could sense it—a quiet, lingering resentment. I had seen something she didn’t want exposed. I had acted where she hadn’t.

So when she spoke loudly about hating abusers, all I could hear was the hypocrisy.

She could talk about protecting children.
But when it came to mine, there was no outrage.
No apology.
No accountability.

Living in that house, I felt the same old truth press down on me:

I was useful as long as I was silent, obedient, and grateful for crumbs.

The moment I insisted on fairness, safety, or honesty, I became a problem.

And problems, in their world, were either punished, underpaid, or pushed out.

37

CHAPTER 37

BROKEN PROMISES, FALSE ACCUSATIONS, AND CONTROL

Peter had promised Happy something small, but to her, it meant the world.

He had said he would take her to the crèche. She clung to that promise with the pure excitement only a child can have. She counted down the time, talked about it, imagined it.

Then the day came.

And Peter didn't.

No call. No explanation. No apology. Just silence.

Happy cried, her little heart broken in a way I couldn't fix with my arms or my words. Watching her wait for someone who didn't show up reopened scars inside me too.

I decided to call him.

I wasn't trying to pick a fight. I just wanted him to understand the effect his broken promise had on his daughter. But when I dialed his number, it wasn't Peter who answered.

It was his wife.

I calmly explained that Peter had promised to take Happy to crèche and hadn't shown up. I told her how Happy had been crying. I wasn't accusing—just stating what had happened.

Her response was instant and hostile.

She spoke to me like I was the problem. Like I was the one stirring drama. As if calling attention to Peter's own words and actions was some kind of crime.

At that moment, I was with Miss Thandeka.

Hearing the way Peter's wife spoke to me, and seeing how small and hesitant I became, Miss Thandeka took the phone from my hand. For once, someone stood up for me. She challenged Peter's wife, spoke firmly on my behalf.

For a brief moment, I felt something I rarely felt: defended.

But that moment didn't last.

The conversation took a dark, shocking turn when Peter's wife made an accusation that struck at the very core of my being.

She claimed I had tried to get Peter arrested by falsely accusing him of raping our child.

Her voice was full of venom as she said it, as if she were the victim. As if my existence was a threat to her image, her comfort, her control.

Her words were not just lies—they were an attack on my integrity as a mother.

I knew the truth.

I knew what had actually happened. I had carried the weight of that truth in silence, not because it didn't matter, but because it mattered too much.

I stayed silent about Happy's case to protect her.

I didn't want people prying into something so painful and private. I didn't want questions whispered behind our backs. I didn't want anyone using her trauma as gossip material or a weapon.

But while I was protecting her in silence, Peter was working in the shadows.

He began spreading a story that I was a liar. That I had tried to destroy his life. That I invented things.

His lies wrapped around us like chains I couldn't cut.

People repeated his version. They whispered. They judged.
The false accusations followed me everywhere, like a bad smell I couldn't wash off.

Meanwhile, the memory of what had truly happened to Happy never left me.

It haunted my days and filled my nights. I would wake up in the dark, heart pounding, the old fear heavy in my chest. I carried a secret that burned, while he carried a lie that spread.

At the same time, another mask was slowly slipping.

The kindness Miss Thandeka had shown at the beginning began to fade. Her "defence" of me over the phone became a brief exception, not the rule.

Her true nature began to emerge.

She became sharp, critical, and controlling. She nitpicked everything I did—how I cleaned, how I moved, how I parented. Nothing was good enough.

Her control even extended to my belongings.

She started burning my things.

She said they were old, useless, not worth keeping. But to me, they weren't just objects. They were what little I owned. Each item she burned felt like another piece of my identity going up in smoke.

There was no respect. No sense that I, too, had a right to space, to privacy, to things that were mine.

She invited her friends over often.

They would gather in the living room, talking and laughing. I always felt their eyes on me—even when I was in another room. Their whispers were not subtle. Their laughter wasn't kind.

One morning, I woke up to find them already there.

They were talking about me, and they weren't trying very hard to hide it. Their tone said everything: ridicule, judgment, contempt.

Miss Thandeka joined in.

She didn't defend me. She didn't correct them. She became part of the chorus, laughing about me in the same house where I scrubbed, worked, and tried to raise my child.

But I kept going.

Despite the emotional abuse, the disrespect, and the constant feeling of being unwelcome in a place I was helping to maintain, I kept working.

I took any piece job I could get.

One day, I got work washing clothes for a man in a wheelchair.

He told me he received a disability grant and assured me he would pay me fairly for my labour. I believed him. I bent over buckets and basins, washed and rinsed until my hands ached.

When the work was done, I asked for my pay.

His face changed.

He waved his hand dismissively and told me to "forget about it." Just like that, my effort, my time, my aching body—dismissed as nothing.

Then he added insult to theft.

He turned his frustration toward my identity. He called me a

"foreigner," spat out the word like poison, and sneered that I probably thought South Africa was a land flowing with milk and honey.

As if my suffering was some joke.
As if my struggle was a choice.
As if I had come searching for comfort and luxury, instead of running from hardship, trying to survive.

I went home crushed.

I told my neighbour—the one who often watched Happy when I went to work—what had happened. She was shocked and angry on my behalf. Even she couldn't believe someone would be so cruel and dishonest.

But cruelty had become a pattern in my life.

Sometimes, late at night, a dark question would slip into my thoughts:

Am I cursed?

Has God turned His face away from me? Why did I keep ending up in the hands of people who saw my vulnerability as an invitation to exploit, insult, and deceive me?

Back at home, things with Miss Thandeka and her husband only grew worse.

Her insults became sharper. Her control more suffocating. Her stress became my burden. And in that cramped space, with my child beside me, I felt once more like I was trapped in a cycle I could not break.

People spoke loudly about being “against abuse” and loving children.

But behind closed doors, their actions told a very different story.

And I was the one who kept paying the price.

38

CHAPTER 38

WHEN KINDNESS IS A CAGE: CONTROL, HUMILIATION, AND FALSE ACCUSATIONS

When I first moved into Miss Thandeka's home, her yard was wild and overgrown.

Weeds choked the ground. Dust and dirt clung to every corner. I saw chaos where there should have been a home. Slowly, I started to clean—pulling weeds, sweeping, and trying to carve out a small, safe space where my daughter, Happy, could play. Bit by bit, the yard changed.

I made a tiny play area for Happy, a piece of childhood in a life that had already seen too much pain. She had only a few toys, but to her, they were treasures.

To Miss Thandeka, they were "dirt."

She complained that Happy's toys made the yard look messy. This, from a woman whose yard had been in complete disarray when I first arrived.

To keep the peace, I did something that broke my own heart.

I burned my daughter's toys.

The little symbols of joy she had clung to—gone in flames because one woman refused to allow them in her yard or even inside the cramped shack we called home.

That moment marked a turning point.

From then on, the atmosphere in that place grew heavier, especially as payday came closer. The closer it got to the day she was supposed to pay me, the more tense and unpleasant things became.

Her moods were unpredictable.

One minute she seemed almost normal, the next she was hostile and cruel. The simple act of receiving my small wage became something I dreaded.

She would use those moments to bully me.

She spoke with no filter, no kindness, no respect. She criticised everything. The way I worked. The way I moved. The way I lived. She often boasted about how strong she was and how she could "deal with" people, even threatening violence toward others.

I lived in a constant state of fear and anxiety.

One day stands out clearly in my mind.

I had just finished a huge load of washing—mountains of clothes. My hands were sore, raw, and swollen from the work. Before the job, I had washed a few of my own clothes and folded them neatly on a dish, planning to put them away later.

When she came home, something strange happened.

For no reason that made any sense, she took my clean clothes, mixed them into a pile of dirty laundry, and shoved them into a plastic bag.

By the time I found them, they smelled terrible. I had to wash them all over again.

It was not an accident.

It was a message: nothing that belonged to me would be treated with care or respect in that space.

And it didn't happen just once.

Whenever she was home, she would obsessively reclean and rearrange everything in the house, even after I had just cleaned.

In the process, some of my small belongings would go "missing," adding another layer of stress and uncertainty.

I could never relax.

Nothing I did was ever enough. My attempts to make the place clean and livable for my child were constantly undermined.

What hurt most was the contrast.

When I arrived, her home was filthy—dusty, neglected, and with piles of dirt hidden behind the door. I had poured real effort into transforming it. But instead of gratitude, there were only criticisms and complaints.

Her behaviour slid from difficult to openly manipulative.

She started deliberately hiding important items in the house, creating stress and confusion. I often overheard her speaking badly about me to others, twisting my actions, making me out to be lazy or ungrateful.

I learned to keep my face calm, to swallow my reactions.

I recognised the tactic. I had seen it before in other homes: emotional control through humiliation and blame.

She began accusing me of breaking household items.

The television. The bed. The sofas.

Things I had never mishandled. Things that were clearly damaged by her own family's carelessness. Still, she pinned the blame on me.

There was no logic behind it—only control.

The public humiliation was the final layer.

At a party we attended, I found out she had been telling everyone that I was useless and dirty. That I didn't clean the yard.

But the funny thing about lies is that sometimes, they betray themselves.

The same people she complained to had seen the yard before and after I arrived. They had witnessed the difference. Some quietly pulled me aside to acknowledge the work I'd done, telling me they knew the truth.

She refused to.

As life grew heavier under that roof, I began quietly looking for a way out.

I knew I couldn't stay there forever. My spirit was being crushed a little more each day. I told myself that I needed to leave before things got worse—before the emotional abuse escalated into something I couldn't recover from.

The very month I decided to leave, everything exploded.

One day, Miss Thandeka came home while I was speaking with a friend. I greeted her.

She ignored me.

I went back to cleaning the room, trying not to let it affect me. But she followed me, her anger following like a storm.

Without a word of thanks or even basic respect, she threw my wages at me.

Then she told me I would no longer be cleaning her yard.

At that moment, everything clicked.

The payday tension. The shifting moods. The resentment.

My pay was the trigger. The fact that she had to give me money for my labour fueled her hostility.

I carefully asked if her cancelling the job meant I also had to leave the shack.

She quickly denied it, pretending to be reasonable. She said she wasn't chasing me away—just stopping the yard work.

But I knew better.

I had seen this pattern before. Once the work stops, the roof follows. And even if she didn't throw me out that second, the emotional violence had already evicted my peace.

I decided: I was leaving. Whether she admitted it or not.

Later that day, Mr. Victor came by, while I was away,likely to check how I was doing.

What happened stunned even me.

Mr. Sithole confronted him and said they no longer wanted me there, that I had to leave. Then he added a vile, false accusation.

He claimed I had asked him for South African ID documents in exchange for sexual favours.

I was horrified.

Not only was this a complete lie, but it completely flipped the truth. He was the one who had made inappropriate advances toward me, not the other way around.

Shaken and disgusted, I went back to the shack.

Miss Thandeka wasn't there. A neighbour told me she had stormed out after a fight with her husband. Not long after, Mr. Sithole told me he'd be leaving the next day.

That's when fear really kicked in.

If he was leaving soon, why stay even one more night? What was he capable of in that time? He'd already lied about me.

What else could he do and then twist the story in his favour?

I felt a cold, heavy sense of danger.

I tried to make sense to Mr. Victor about everything— the lies, the accusation, and my fear. He confronted Mr. Sithole directly.

At first, the man denied everything.

But there were witnesses. People had heard what he said to Mr. Victor. Faced with the truth, his arrogance cracked.

He eventually apologised.

But his apology felt forced, thin, and empty. Words spoken for survival, not from remorse. I had to leave their home the very same day.

The next day, one of Miss Thandeka's friends called me. Her voice was sharp, demanding to know what I had done to him.

I explained the truth—carefully, honestly—about his lies and my fear.

She didn't want the truth.

She wanted a story that made sense within her loyalty to Miss
Thandeka. She twisted my words and then went around telling people that I had insulted her.

What I had hoped would be a step toward freedom—leaving their home—turned into a fresh wave of problems.

Their lies followed me out into the community.

One by one, my piece jobs disappeared. The people I had worked for started looking at me differently.

When asked about my sudden departure, Mr. Sithole told anyone who would listen that I had accused him of attempted rape, and that he'd been forced to throw me out.

To make himself look noble, he added that I had later apologised—but he, being so "good," decided he no longer wanted me near his property.

His lie made me the villain in a story where I had only ever been the one trying to survive.

Once again, I was left to face the wreckage:
No work.
Damaged reputation.
Another home lost.
Another community turned cold.

But even as their stories spread, one thing didn't change:

The truth.

It lived in me. It burned in my memory. It survived their lies.

And as long as I carried that truth, there was still a part of me they could not touch, twist, or own.

39

CHAPTER 39

THE IRON IN MY SOUL: FROM TEARS TO TIMBER

After my business was stolen, the world watched me fall.

I went from being a shop owner to a wanderer, drifting from place to place, relying on the same community that had seen my rise to now witness my struggle. The hands that reached out to "help" often had hidden motives—hands that pulled me deeper into dependency, control, and humiliation.

I became a collector of tins.
A carrier of scrap.
A beggar at gates where I was once greeted as a customer or neighbour.

My name became a joke.

They used my story to spice up gossip, to build shallow friendships on the back of my suffering. I was the cautionary tale, the punchline, the example of "how far someone can fall."

But while they were talking, I was working.
While they were laughing, my daughter was eating.

I felt like an orphan in a crowded world—surrounded by people, yet truly belonging nowhere.

Still, I knew one thing with absolute certainty:
As long as I was breathing, hunger would not sleep in our bed.

FROM TEARS TO TIMBER

There is a specific kind of strength that is born when you run out of tears.

I remember the day the wind came and tore my shack apart. It ripped through the yard, lifted the sheets of iron, and scattered the pieces of my home across the dirt like they were nothing.

Once, that would have broken me.

But as I stood there, watching the ruins of yet another "home" lying in pieces, I realised my face was dry. The part of me that used to weep endlessly had been replaced by something else:

Iron.

A raw, unyielding power had taken the place of tears. I didn't collapse. I didn't beg. I didn't look around for someone to come and fix it for me.

I didn't need a man to rebuild the walls.

I became the mother and the father. I stepped fully into the role Peter had abandoned—not just emotionally, but practically. The energy I once spent on crying, I redirected into hammering, lifting, planning, hustling.

I began to build—not just a shack, but a life.

THE ARCHITECT OF A NEW LIFE

Every tin I collected, every piece job I took, every insult I survived—I turned it all into building material.

I realised I was not just surviving. I was building.

Not a house of wood and corrugated iron, but a house of character.

I came to see that my name—dragged through every conversation, twisted in every rumour—was not a curse.

It was a badge.

If people needed to talk about me to feel important, it only proved how much space I occupied in their minds. If my struggle was their entertainment, then my resilience was their unseen mirror.

I am still building.

The work is not finished. The scars on my back still ache, and some days the memories press hard against my chest. But I am no longer drowning.

I have surfaced.

I have taken the very stones they threw at me and laid them, one by one, into the foundation of a different future.

A future where my daughter never has to know the level of embarrassment I endured.

A future where my worth is not measured by someone else's gossip or approval.

A future I am actively designing, piece by piece.

I am no longer just a scavenger.
No longer just a victim.
No longer just a survivor.

I am the architect of a life that belongs to me.

40

CHAPTER 40

REFLECTION FOR THE READER

This final chapter is the emotional climax of my memoir.

It is not here to say, “Look how strong I am because I never felt pain.” No. It is here to show you that strength is not the absence of pain—it is what you do while you are in pain.

It is the decision to build when everything around you has been broken.

It is choosing dignity when others try to take it away.

It is feeding your child on the same streets where they laughed at you.

When I became "Happy's mother and father," I reclaimed a power that many tried to take from me.

Miss Louis tried to destroy my name.
Miss Mclony tried to break my body and my spirit.
Others tried to buy, define, and control me.

But even when they took my business, they could not take my
"man power"—the inner strength, courage, and determination to stand, build, and keep moving.

That is the iron in my soul.

And if you are holding this story in your hands, know this:

You, too, can take what was meant to break
you and use it as timber for the life you
decide to build next.

Afterword

A FINAL WORD

The Beauty of the Build

If you are reading this and you feel like the wind has taken everything you've worked for, I want you to look at your hands.

They may be tired.
They may be scared.
But they are still yours.

For a long time, I believed that my story was written by the people who hurt me. I believed the lies told by neighbours and the insults shouted in the street. I thought that being "cast out" meant I was worth nothing.

But I have learned something the hard way:

The world cannot break what it did not build.

They took my business, but they couldn't take my mind.
They bruised my back, but they couldn't reach my soul.

And while they were busy trying to tear me down, I was busy becoming the mother and the father my daughter needed.

I am no longer a "street kid."
I am no longer just a victim of the compound.

I am an architect.
I am an author.
I am a survivor.

To every woman who is currently a human shield for her children:

Do not let the embarrassment drown you.

Your tears are not a sign of weakness; they are the water that will help your new life grow.

Keep building.
Keep walking.

The iron is already inside you.

With love and strength,
Samukeliso Moyo

About the Author

Samukeliso Moyo was born in Matopo, Kezi, Zimbabwe. She attended Goholi Primary School and Goholl Secondary School, and is the first born of three children. From a young age, she found comfort and courage in words, often writing stories long before she ever dreamed of publishing a book.

FROM STRUGGLE TO STRENGTH is her first book.

Today, Samukeliso is an author, independent publisher, and the visionary creator of The Sibanda Iron Soul Series™. She crafts stories that act as a bridge between hardship and healing, drawing deeply from her own lived experiences.

Having walked through some of life's harshest "forges," she writes with raw honesty and a clear mission: to help readers turn their struggles into enduring strength. As a devoted mother and a quiet advocate for personal growth in her community, she believes every soul carries an indestructible core that can be polished into a crown of purpose.

When she is not developing new projects for the series, Samukeliso connects with a growing community of readers on Facebook, sharing reflections on resilience, faith, and the ongoing journey toward a more joyful, grounded life.

www.ingramcontent.com/pod-product-compliance
Lightning Source LLC
LaVergne TN
LVHW010605100826
845148LV00014B/2850